CW00405567

SE 5a
VS
ALBATROS D V

Western Front 1917–18

JON GUTTMAN

First published in Great Britain in 2009 by Osprey Publishing,
Midland House, West Way, Botley, Oxford OX2 0PH, UK
443 Park Avenue South, New York, NY 10016, USA
E-mail: info@ospreypublishing.com

© 2009 Osprey Publishing Ltd

All rights reserved. Apart from any fair dealing for the purpose of private study, research,
criticism or review, as permitted under the Copyright, Designs and Patents Act, 1988, no part
of this publication may be reproduced, stored in a retrieval system, or transmitted in any form
or by any means, electronic, electrical, chemical, mechanical, optical, photocopying, recording
or otherwise, without the prior written permission of the copyright owner. Enquiries should
be addressed to the Publishers.

A CIP catalogue record for this book is available from the British Library

ISBN: 978 1 84603 471 8
PDF e-book ISBN: 978 1 84908 118 4

Edited by Tony Holmes
Cover artwork, cockpit and armament scrap views by Jim Laurier
Three-views by Harry Dempsey
Battlescene by Mark Postlethwaite
Page layout by Ken Vail Graphic Design, Cambridge, UK
Index by Alison Worthington
Typeset in ITC Conduit and Adobe Garamond
Maps by Bounford.com
Originated by PDQ Digital Media Solutions, Suffolk, UK
Printed in China through Bookbuilders

09 10 11 12 13 10 9 8 7 6 5 4 3 2 1

FOR A CATALOGUE OF ALL BOOKS PUBLISHED BY OSPREY
MILITARY AND AVIATION PLEASE CONTACT:

Osprey Direct, c/o Random House Distribution Center,
400 Hahn Road, Westminster, MD 21157
Email: uscustomerservice@ospreypublishing.com

Osprey Direct, The Book Service Ltd, Distribution Centre,
Colchester Road, Frating Green, Colchester, Essex, CO7 7DW
E-mail: customerservice@ospreypublishing.com

www.ospreypublishing.com

German ranks	French ranks	USAS ranks	RFC/RAF ranks
Rittmeister (Rittm)	Cavalry Captain	Cavalry Captain	Cavalry Captain
Hauptmann (Hptm)	Capitaine	Captain	Army Captain
Oberleutnant (Oblt)	Lieutenant	First Lieutenant	Lieutenant
Leutnant (Ltn)	Sous-Lieutenant	Second Lieutenant	Second Lieutenant
Offizierstellvertreter (OffzSt)	Adjutant	Warrant Officer	Warrant Officer
Feldwebel	Sergent-Chef	Master Sergeant	Master Sergeant
Vizefeldwebel (Vzfw)	Maréchal-des-Logis	Sergeant 1st Class	Sergeant 1st Class
Sergeant	Sergent	Sergeant	Sergeant
Unteroffizier (Uffz)	Caporal	Corporal	Corporal
Gefreiter (Gfr)	Brigadier	Private 1st Class	Private 1st Class
Flieger (Flgr)	Soldat	Private	Private

Editor's Note

For ease of comparison between types, imperial
measurements are used almost exclusively throughout this
book. The exception is weapon calibres, which are given in
their official designation, whether metric or imperial. The
following data will help in converting the imperial
measurements to metric:

1 mile = 1.6km
1lb = 0.45kg
1 yard = 0.9m
1ft = 0.3m
1in. = 2.54cm/25.4mm
1 gal = 4.5 litres
1 ton (US) = 0.9 tonnes
1hp = 0.74kW

Acknowledgements

Thanks to Alex Imrie, Alex Revell and Greg
VanWyngarden, as well as the late Walter C. Daniel,
Gwilym H. Lewis, Robert Leslie Chidlaw-Roberts and
Hans-Georg von der Osten for their assistance in
preparing this volume.

Cover Art

The third SE 5a-equipped unit, No. 84 Sqn, had been
in action for just two weeks when, on 31 October 1917,
Capt Kenneth M. St C. G. Leask in Vickers-built B579
and five aeroplanes from his A Flight attacked four
German aircraft, only to be jumped by 12 more. In the
ensuing melee Leask and 2Lt John Steele Ralston, in
B4853, were credited with sending down Albatros D Vs
out of control over Menin at 1540 hrs. This was Leask's
third victory of an eventual eight and Ralston's second of
twelve. However, 2Lts Edward W. Powell and George R.
Gray failed to return. Powell may have been killed by
Ltn Heinrich Bongartz of *Jasta* 36, who claimed an SE 5a
south of Roulers at 1610 hrs (German time). This was his
third victory of the day, and his 20th in an overall tally of
33. Gray had dived on Albatros D Vs of *Jasta* 'Boelcke',
whose commander, Ltn d R Erwin Böhme, climbed to
confront him, then eluded four or five attacks by Gray.
'At the same time he gradually began to lose height',
Böhme noted, 'and at an opportune moment I turned
the tables on him'. The Germans recovered SE 5a B544
roughly intact, but Gray died of his wounds, having been
the 21st of 24 victories for Böhme prior to his own fiery
demise on 29 November 1917. (Artwork by Jim Laurier)

CONTENTS

INTRODUCTION

Amid the ongoing quest for aerial superiority during World War I, the late spring of 1917 saw two competing attempts to refine proven designs. The Royal Aircraft Factory SE 5a incorporated improvements to the original SE 5 airframe, along with an extra 50hp, to produce a fast and reliable 'ace-maker' that proved to be a formidable adversary for German fighter pilots right through to the end of the war. The Albatros D V, a sleeker-looking development of the deadly D III of 'Bloody April' notoriety, was a more disappointing design, for it suffered a rash of lower wing failures once in service at the front.

The SE 5 that entered combat during April 1917 was a curious mix of conservatism and misguided attempts at innovation. Structurally, its airframe was little different from the prewar Blériot Experimental BE 2, though its overall layout certainly made a difference in combat. The SE 5 was the first British single-seat fighter to mount two machine guns, although the Sopwith Camel was the first to mount twin weapons. Hedging its bets, the Royal Aircraft Factory combined a synchronised Vickers machine gun in the fuselage with a Lewis firing over the propeller arc by means of a Foster mount on the upper wing – a versatile arrangement, perhaps, but one that found little favour in the frontline. And although the pilot had an adjustable armoured seat and a semi-enclosed cockpit, these refinements only added weight and drag at the expense of performance.

Fortunately for the RFC, one of the new fighter's recipients, Capt Albert Ball, did more than complain about its shortcomings. An inveterate tinkerer, he set about changing what he thought was wrong with the scout, and many of his custom touches were incorporated in improved versions of the SE 5 just as No 56 Sqn was blooding the fighter in France. Further improvements based on field experience, combined with an additional 50hp, subsequently turned the reasonably good SE 5 into the superb SE 5a.

By the late summer of 1917, SE 5as from Nos 56 and 60 Sqn were starting to show the fighter's potential over the Western Front, and more units were either forming or in the process of being re-equipped with the scout, powered either by French- or British-made variants of the geared 200hp Hispano Suiza 8B engine or the direct-drive 200hp Wolsleley W4A Viper. These joined Sopwith Pups and Camels, AIRCO DH 5s, Nieuport sesquiplanes and Bristol F 2B two-seat fighters on a succession of offensive patrols (OPs) into German territory.

Restricted only by weather, these flights seemed to lack any purpose other than to lay claim to the sky they currently occupied. This policy, promulgated by the Royal Flying Corps (RFC) high command under Maj Gen Hugh Montague Trenchard, was intended to maintain high morale among the British while downgrading it among the Germans. Such an attitude was apt for the general Allied trend of 1917, marked by a series of offensives on the Western Front that sought to achieve the breakthrough that would win the war.

In direct contrast, Germany's stance on the Western Front throughout 1917 was primarily defensive, thus containing, or at least limiting, Allied gains there, while focusing its offensive effort towards knocking the eastern threats posed by Rumania and Russia out of the conflict. The German *Jagdstafflen*, or fighter squadrons, acted well in line with that strategy, employing tactics that sought to challenge Allied intrusions on their terms with a minimal expenditure in fuel, materiel and trained personnel – resources that were all far more limited for the Central Powers than for their Allied adversaries.

SE 5 A4850 shows the custom touches applied by Capt Albert Ball, No. 56 Sqn's A Flight commander prior to the unit heading to France in April 1917. Many of these modifications were subsequently incorporated into production SE 5s to the type's betterment. Ball went on to be the first of about a hundred pilots to 'make ace' flying the SE 5/5a during the course of World War I. (Alex Revell)

An evocative – and suitably colourful – line-up of 12 Albatros D Vs and two D IIIs assigned to *Jasta* 5 at Boistrancourt in late July 1917. The third aeroplane from the foreground, with a green fuselage and red-bordered black and white chequers, as well as *Jasta* 5's red nose and green tail, trimmed in red, was flown by ace Vfw Otto Könnecke. (Greg VanWyngarden).

While SE 5a pilots on OPs faced problems endemic to carrying out their missions in enemy territory, such as the prevailing wind usually being against them on the return leg of their flights, their foes in Albatros D Vs were primarily engaged in working around the inherent shortcomings of their own aircraft. All other factors being equal, the SE 5a was intrinsically the better aeroplane. Although less manoeuvrable than the Albatros, it was faster in level flight and excelled in a dive, whereas the D V pilot had always to be mindful of the very real possibility of his single-spar lower wing tearing loose.

With their respective measures thus taken, throughout the summer and autumn of 1917, the SE 5a and Albatros D V units squared off for some of the year's most intense aerial contests over such key Allied objectives as Messines Ridge, Ypres, Passchendaele and Cambrai. That the German *Jagdflieger* continued to take the toll they did on the RFC at that time was regarded – on both sides – as a reflection of their skill and cunning, rather than the quality of the aeroplane in which they had to take on all Allied comers.

While the SE 5a shared the sky with a variety of other British and French fighter types, German pleas for an Albatros D V replacement resulted in it being joined by Pfalz D III biplanes and Fokker Dr I triplanes from the autumn of 1917. Neither type proved to be entirely satisfactory, however, with the Pfalz being judged more sluggish than the Albatros in aerial combat and the triplane slower. As a result of these shortcomings, both types were produced in numbers that supplemented, rather than replaced, the D V.

In the autumn of 1917, efforts to reinforce the Albatros D V's structure and increase the compression and output of its Mercedes engine produced the D Va, which somewhat, but never fully, alleviated the flaws intrinsic to its sesquiplane wing configuration. Nevertheless, pending deliveries in quantity of the superb new Fokker D VII in the spring of 1918, Albatrosen were the most numerically important fighters available when the Germans launched their final offensive on 21 March 1918. And in spite of the scout's shortcomings, German tactics and piloting skill meant that the Albatros D Va remained a dangerous foe that aviators flying the SE 5a dismissed at their peril.

A good many Germans who mastered the Albatros D V and managed to survive the fighting over the Somme and Flanders in 1917 went on to truly excel when the Fokker D VII arrived in 1918. It is of more than a little significance though, that even in the new Fokker, they had their hands just as full tackling the still-formidable SE 5a as they had had when flying the old Albatros.

Viewed in historic hindsight, both the SE 5a and Albatros D V share an image as the workhorses of their respective fighter arms during the second half of 1917, dominating the growing aerial encounters of that period as their unfairly more famous stablemates, the Sopwith Camel and Fokker Dr I triplane, would those of the first half of 1918.

If the aircraft were relatively prosaic, however, posterity's remembrance of the SE 5a and the Albatros are richly coloured by the men who flew them. As renowned as Achilles, Diomedes, Hector and Aeneas – at least to Britons – are the names of Albert Ball, Jimmy McCudden, Arthur P. F. Rhys Davids and Richard Aveline Maybery, as well as Manfred von Richthofen, Erwin Böhme, Fritz Rumey and the once-anonymous, but outstanding, Albatros pilot that McCudden immortalised as 'Greentail', Otto Könnecke. The Albatros, for that matter, has enjoyed a literally colourful image thanks to the kaleidoscope of unit and individual schemes that the Germans gave them. Aside from a few short-lived and officially disapproved-of forays into similar décor, the SE 5/5a's colourful reputation lies not in its appearance, but in the heroic deeds perpetrated by the occupants of its cockpit.

Albatros D Vs of *Jasta* 3 at Wyngene aerodrome in the winter of 1917–18. The markings worn by the scouts seem to have been strictly personal, including D.4460/17 *Hilde* in the foreground, flown by Ltn Joahim Rogalla von Bieberstein, and the 'M'-marked machine at left, probably camouflaged in patches of olive green, brown and mauve, flown by Ltn Karl Menckhoff. (Greg VanWyngarden)

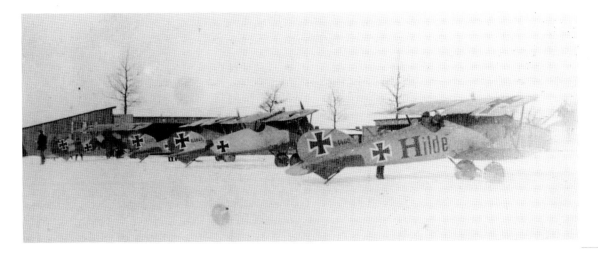

CHRONOLOGY

1916

Summer John Kenworthy and Henry P. Folland propose SE 5 design. Robert Thelen's Albatros D I and D II fighter designs are tested and accepted for production.

16 September Albatros D Is and D IIs enter combat with *Jasta* 2, as Ltn Otto Walter Höhne brings down an FE 2b.

17 September Hptm Oswald Boelcke leads *Jasta* 2 in a demonstration of team effort against BE 2cs and FE 2bs that results in five victories, including the first for Ltn Manfred *Freiherr* von Richthofen.

22 November Maj Frank W. Goodden flies prototype SE 5 A4561 for the first time.

28 November First geared 200hp Hispano-Suiza 8B engine delivered to Royal Aircraft Factory.

1917

7 January First Albatros D IIIs arrive at *Jasta* 2.

24 January Ltn Manfred von Richthofen, now commanding *Jasta* 11, suffers lower wing failure, calling attention to the Albatross D III's structural weakness.

28 January Maj Frank W. Goodden killed in second SE 5 prototype A4562.

March No. 56 Sqn equipped with SE 5s at London Colney.

6 April United States declares war on Germany.

7 April No. 56 Sqn flies to Vert Galant, France.

9 April–17 May Battles of Arras and Vimy Ridge precipitate 'Bloody April' for the RFC.

16–20 April Second Battle of the Aisne-Chemin des Dames.

21 April Albatros informs *Idflieg* of its 'lightened Albatros D III airframe' and gets first order for 200 D Vs.

22 April First SE 5 combat sortie.

23 April Capt Albert Ball scores first SE 5 victories.

May First Albatros D Vs arrive at *Jagstaffeln*.

7 May Capt Albert Ball killed in action in SE 5 A4850.

Maj Roderic Stanley Dallas, CO of No. 40 Sqn, flew SE 5a D3511 in an unusual multi-shade camouflage scheme on 28 May 1918. A former naval pilot, Australian-born Dallas' score stood at 32 when he was shot down and killed near Lievin on 1 June by Ltn Hans Werner of *Jasta* 14, flying a Fokker Dr I. (Greg VanWyngarden)

29 May	SE 5a prototype undergoes test flying at Martlesham Heath.
7–14 June	First Battle of Messines Ridge.
23 June	*Luftstreitskräfte* inaugurates *Amerikaprogramm*, designed to double the number of frontline units.
24 June	*Jagdgeschwader* I formed under Rittm Manfred *Frhr* von Richthofen, comprising *Jastas* 4, 6, 10 and 11.
18 July	Manfred von Richthofen writes to *Idflieg* denouncing D V.
31 July	First Battle of Passchendaele begins.
August	*Idflieg* orders first 262 of new, strengthened Albatros D Va.
August	First ten 200hp Wosleley W4A Viper engines produced, which will supplement and ultimately eclipse the Hispano-Suiza in SE 5as.
November	First Sunbeam Arab engine tests in SE 5a, which ultimately prove unsatisfactory.
6 November	First Battle of Passchendaele ends.
20–28 November	British Cambrai Offensive.
30 November	Germans launch counter-offensive at Cambrai.

An Albatros D V sports the blue fuselage, red nose and sky-blue undersides of *Jasta* 18, as well as the personal band of Ltn Arthur Rahn, at Avelines in December 1917. (Greg VanWyngarden).

6 December	German Cambrai counter-offensive concludes.

1918

21 March–5 April	German *Kaiserschlacht* offensive begins in Picardy with Operation *Michael*.
1 April	Royal Flying Corps (RFC) and Royal Naval Air Service (RNAS) combine into Royal Air Force (RAF).
9–29 April	Germans launch Operation *Georgette* (the Battle of the Lys).
23 April	Battle for Kemmel Ridge.
30 April	928 Albatros D Vas, 131 D Vs and 19 Fokker D VIIs at front.
27 May–14 June	Germans launch Aisne offensive with Operation *Blücher*, employing Fokker D VIIs in quantity for the first time.
9 June	Battle of the Matz.
15 July–3 August	Second Battle of the Marne.
8–10 August	Battle of Amiens, which sees SE 5as and Sopwith Camels numerically dominate the RAF inventory, complemented by Bristol F 2Bs and Sopwith Dolphins. Fokker D VII is the principal German fighter, with Albatros D Va still serving a supplementary role along with Pfalz D IIIa and D XII, Roland D VI and SSW D III and D IV.

DESIGN AND DEVELOPMENT

SE 5/5a

Even while the AIRCO DH 2 pusher scout was helping to end the 'Fokker Scourge' by countering Germany's first fighters to be equipped with synchronised machine guns in the summer of 1916, Britain's RFC was aware of the ultimate superiority in performance that tractor biplanes such as the Bristol and Sopwith Scouts had over a pusher. The latter design would always be hampered by its drag-producing latticework structure of struts and wires that held the empennage aft of the engine and propeller. By the time the RFC received its first SPAD VII to evaluate on 9 September 1916, the Royal Aircraft Factory at Farnborough was engaged in designing its own Hispano-Suiza-powered fighter with a synchronised forward-firing machine gun.

In fact, company engineers John Kenworthy, Henry P. Folland and Maj Frank W. Goodden already had two ideas in the works as early as June of that year. One, designated the FE 10 (Farman Experimental No 10), was an impractical-looking contraption with the pilot and his machine gun perched in front of the propeller in a nacelle braced to the undercarriage and upper wing in a manner similar to that used by the gunner of the SPAD A2, the unsuccessful ancestor of the SPAD VII.

The other design, designated SE 5 (Scouting Experimental No 5), was similar in overall layout, but with the engine in front and the pilot seated aft of the wings – essentially a smaller, more compactly proportioned single-seat version of the Royal Aircraft Factory BE 2c. Not surprisingly, the conventional design was selected for further development, but the FE 10's vertical tail surfaces were retained in lieu of the smaller fin and rudder originally conceived for the SE 5.

'It's a pixie!' Maj Frank W. Goodden declared to Henry P. Folland after his first flight in SE 5 prototype A4561 on 22 November 1916. Probably seen at Hounslow in January 1917, A4681 reveals continuing development in the form of a modified windscreen and exhausts. (Greg VanWyngarden)

When the first 21 French-made Hispano-Suiza 8A engines were delivered to the RFC on 20 September, most were slated for installation in license-built SPAD VIIs, but two were used to power the first and second SE 5 prototypes, A4561 and A4562. On 28 November the Royal Aircraft Factory received its first example of the new geared 200hp Hispano-Suiza 8B, which it subsequently installed in the third prototype, A4563, thereby creating the first SE 5a.

SE 5 A4562 broke up during a test flight on 28 January 1917, killing Maj Goodden. Simple modifications corrected the aeroplane's structural problems, however, and the first production SE 5, A4845, cleared its final inspection on 2 March 1917. The first production batch of SE 5s did not make a promising impression on their pilots, who complained of poor lateral control – a shortcoming that was alleviated somewhat, but never entirely, by shortening the wingspan and reducing the rake of the wingtips in later production SE 5s and SE 5as. Early SE 5s featured an overhead gravity tank, a large half-canopy that was soon dubbed 'the greenhouse' and a mechanism that could raise or lower the pilot's seat.

Armament consisted of one 0.303-in. Vickers machine gun faired into the upper left side of the fuselage in front of the cockpit, synchronised by means of a new CC Fire Control Timing Gear. This system had been developed by Maj George B. Colley and Rumanian George Constantinesco, who had come to Britain in 1910. His 'Theory of Sonics' lay the foundation of continuum mechanics – the transmission of power through liquids, gases and solids by means of vibrations or pressure pulses.

The CC gear applied Constantinesco's theory to a hydraulic interrupter gear, which initially used oil. This early version, introduced in the de Havilland DH 4 in March 1917 and subsequently used in the SE 5, was prone to frequent failure. However, a later development, using a mixture of 90 percent paraffin (kerosene) and ten percent oil, eventually proved to be more reliable, and in fact superior to the mechanical interrupter gear that had predominated on both sides of the frontline before it.

For the time being, however, the Royal Aircraft Factory hedged its bets by giving the SE 5 a second weapon in the form of a 0.303-in. Lewis gun on a Foster mount

SE 5s of No. 56 Sqn are lined up at London Colney aerodrome before departing for France on 7 April 1917. (Imperial War Museum Q56015)

on the upper wing that could fire over the propeller, similar to the arrangement on early French Nieuport 11s and RFC Nieuport 17s. This made the SE 5 the first single-seat British fighter designed to use two – albeit not twin – machine guns.

The first SE 5s were assigned to No. 56 Sqn under Maj Richard Graham Blomfield, a new unit that nevertheless had the benefit of a handpicked cadre of experienced pilots, including flight leaders Capts Albert Ball, Cyril M. Crowe and Henry Meintjes. The most famous of Blomfield's 'old hands' was 32-victory ace Ball, an eccentric but brilliantly aggressive loner whose exploits as a Nieuport pilot in No. 60 Sqn were already legendary in the RFC. Ball had high expectations for the SE 5, but after giving the first prototype a ten-minute test flight on 23 November 1916 he remarked with bitter regret that the new scout had 'turned out a dud'.

On 7 April 1917, 13 SE 5s of No. 56 Sqn landed at Vert Galant aerodrome, joining No. 19 Sqn's SPAD VIIs and the Pups of No. 66 Sqn. The unit and its new fighters reached the front at the start of the Battle of Arras, which was a British offensive meant to serve as a diversion for French Gen Robert Nivelle's push, which would be launched along the Aisne on 16 April.

Ball had made no secret of his dislike for the SE 5, and when the RFC's commander Maj Gen Trenchard visited the sector, the ace flew to Le Hameau and entreated him to replace the new fighters with Nieuports. Trenchard lent him a sympathetic ear and Ball went away convinced that the SE 5s would be replaced. Nevertheless, by then the ace had already taken the liberty of modifying his personal machine, A4850, while waiting for No. 56 Sqn's disembarkation orders at London Colney in March.

Ball replaced the 'half-greenhouse' with a small Avro windscreen, which reduced drag and gave the pilot better access to the Lewis gun. He removed the adjustable armoured seat and replaced it with a board until a simpler seat could be installed. The lower slide on the Lewis' Foster mount was lengthened by two inches to make it easier for the pilot to replace the ammunition drums, and Ball discarded his synchronised Vickers gun entirely. He also removed the petrol and water gravity tanks from the

LEFT
A close-up of Capt Albert Ball in his modified SE 5 A4850 shows his Avro windscreen and the complete absence of the Vickers gun forward of the cockpit. Echoing Ball's initial impression of the fighter, future ace Cecil Lewis later declared, 'The SE 5a as the Royal Aircraft Factory turned it out was an abortion. It was the pilots of No. 56 Sqn who turned it into a practical fighter.' (Alex Revell)

BELOW
Also photographed at London Colney on 7 April 1917, Lt Cecil A. Lewis poses beside SE 5 A4853, which was a typical example of the first production batch fitted with the 'half-greenhouse' windscreen. Lewis would score eight victories, all in A4853, and went on to greater fame for his classic book *Sagittarius Rising*, as a 1938 Academy Award-winning screenplay writer and a founding father of the BBC, among other things. (Jon Guttman)

upper wing and installed long SPAD-type exhaust pipes to the engine. Finally, an extra Lewis gun was installed, firing downwards through the floor of the cockpit. Ball noted that his alterations resulted in a considerable improvement in performance, although he still considered the SE 5 to be 'a rotten machine'.

Not all of Ball's modifications met with RFC approval, with the obliquely mounted downward-firing Lewis gun deemed to be a bad idea. The Royal Aircraft Factory adopted many of the ace's revisions for future production aircraft, however, and the SE 5 was the better for it. The undercarriage wheels were also moved further forward and the external overwing tank replaced by internally fitted fuel and water gravity tanks behind the leading edge of the upper wing centre section. The latter was also strengthened and covered with plywood to withstand the Lewis gun's recoil.

Snow and bad weather delayed test flying in the modified aircraft until 13 April. That afternoon, Ball learned that Trenchard had authorised him a Nieuport for his personal use, although he still had to fly his SE 5 on squadron patrols. Ball was delighted, and that evening South African Capt Meintjes flew Nieuport 17 Scout B1522 in from Candas, while Ball brought back his modified SE 5.

No. 56 Sqn despatched its first operational patrol at 1018 hrs on 22 April, the pilots' enthusiasm being somewhat tempered by orders that they were on no account to cross the frontlines. Ball led his A Flight in A4850, but Lt Gerald J. C. Maxwell developed engine trouble due to oil

Some of No. 56 Sqn's initial complement gather for a photograph at London Colney prior to heading for France. Standing, from left to right, are Lt Gerald J. C. Maxwell, 2Lt William B. Melville, Lt Henry M. T. Lehmann, Lt Clarence R. W. Knight, Lt Leonard M. Barlow and 2Lt Kenneth J. Knaggs. Seated, again from left to right, are Lt Cecil A. Lewis, Lt John O. Leach, Maj Richard G. Blomfield, Capt Albert Ball and 2Lt Reginald T. C. Hoidge. (Greg VanWyngarden)

OVERLEAF
SE 5a B2 of Capt Geoffrey H. 'Beery' Bowman, No. 56 Sqn, based at Droglandt in December 1917. Born on 2 May 1891, Bowman had served in the Royal Warwickshire Regiment before joining the RFC on 20 March 1916. He scored his first two victories in DH 2s with No. 29 Sqn, and was then posted to No. 56 Sqn as C Flight leader. Bowman had added 11 victories to his tally in SE 5 A8900 by 27 July. He downed another eight enemy aeroplanes – all Albatros D Vs – in SE 5a B2 between 17 August and 23 December 1917, but on Christmas Day the fighter was written off in a crash whilst being flown by fellow ace Capt Louis W. Jarvis. On 6 February 1918 Maj Bowman was made CO of No. 41 Sqn, with whom he scored his last eight victories, for a total of 32. Retiring from the RAF in December 1941, Bowman died on 25 March 1970.

circulation failure and had to drop out. At 11,000ft, Ball spotted an Albatros two-seater over Adinfer, and although he fired three drums of ammunition into it at ranges as close as 150ft, the German managed to dive away. Another enemy aeroplane was seen at noon, but it was too far away to engage. 'Duke' Meintjes led C Flight on a second fruitless patrol that afternoon.

Capt Crowe led the squadron's first offensive patrol the next morning – St George's Day – but encountered no enemy aeroplanes. Ball, meanwhile, had taken off alone in his Nieuport at 0600 hrs, hoping to catch German aircraft en route to or from their aerodromes at Douai or Cambrai. Two Albatros C two-seaters duly appeared at 8,000ft over Cambrai and Ball carried out his usual tactic – a dive and then a pullout, at which point he pulled up his wing-mounted Lewis gun and fired at his quarry from below. The first German eluded him, but Ball slipped under the second, fired half a drum of Lewis into it and then pursued his diving prey until it crashed near the road between Tilloy and Abancourt. Thus, No. 56 Sqn's first official victory was not scored in its officially authorised aircraft!

Ball dived on another Albatros C a few minutes later, but its pilot throttled back, causing him to overshoot. With the tables thus turned, the German observer put 15 bullets through Ball's lower wing spar. The ace dived away and landed safely at 0845 hrs. The Nieuport's lower wing had to be replaced, however, forcing him to fly his second patrol of the day in his unloved SE 5.

Taking off at 1045 hrs and climbing to 12,000ft, Ball attacked an Albatros C III over Adinfer, only to suffer a gun jam. After landing to clear his weapon at Le Hameau aerodrome and then resuming his patrol, at 1145 hrs he sighted five Albatros D IIIs over Sevigny and again dived, firing 150 rounds into one opponent, which fell out of control and burst into flames before hitting the ground. The remaining four German aircraft put some rounds into Ball's aeroplane, but he used the SE 5's superior diving speed to escape. Three-quarters of an hour later, Ball encountered yet another Albatros C III north of Cambrai, dived underneath it and fired half a drum of Lewis into the

14

machine's belly. Its pilot, Vfw Egert of *Flieger Abteilung (Fl Abt) 7*, retired in a steep dive, made a good landing and then aided his observer, Ltn Berger, who had suffered a severe neck wound.

Meintjes led a five-aeroplane patrol at 1315 hrs that afternoon, but 30 minutes later Lt William B. Melville turned back with engine trouble and his SE 5, A4852, overturned while landing. The rest of the flight chased a German two-seater south of Lens but failed to bring it down. In the final sortie of the day, Ball led 2Lts Clarence R. W. Knight and John O. Leach in search of enemy balloons, but they returned empty-handed at 1735 hrs.

So ended the SE 5's first 48 hours in combat. Only the redoubtable Ball had shot anything down, but squadron morale was high nevertheless.

During one of several combats on the 24th, 2Lt Maurice A. Kay and Lt Leonard M. Barlow both suffered jammed Vickers but used their Lewis guns to press home their attacks on two two-seaters. Aided by Crowe, they brought one aircraft down near Bellone, whose crew, from *Flieger Abteilung (Artillerie) (Fl Abt (A))* 224, survived. Crowe, whose Vickers also jammed, and Kay subsequently engaged some red-marked Albatros D IIIs with their Lewises in No. 56 Sqn's first, but hardly last, run-in with von Richthofen's *Jasta* 11.

Although the results achieved in these early actions had been disappointing for the unit, the SE 5s had not done badly. Even Ball came to appreciate the modified fighter, and used it to add 11 victories in his final total of 44. Inevitably, the squadron suffered its first fatality on 30 April when Kay was shot down east of Fresnoy by Ltn Edmund Nathanael of *Jasta* 5, after which Leach claimed to have despatched Kay's killer in flames, in spite of *Jasta* 5 suffering no losses that day.

A far more serious blow to No. 56 Sqn's morale occurred on 7 May when it lost two flight commanders. After downing an Albatros D III in concert with Lts Melville, Cecil A. Lewis and Reginald T. C. Hoidge, followed by a solo victory that probably wounded Ltn Wofgang Plüschow of *Jasta* 11, Meintjes was outmanoeuvred by a third D III pilot who shot off the top of his control column and wounded him in the wrist. Meintjes dived away and managed to land near the headquarters of the British Army's 46th Division before passing out from loss of blood. The South African's score stood at eight, but he was out of the war.

Soon after that Albert Ball went missing. Although early German propaganda credited his demise to Ltn Lothar von Richthofen – the Red Baron's brother in

The original German marker erected at the first SE 5 ace's grave reads, 'Fallen in air battle for his fatherland, English flier Capt Albert Ball, Royal Flying Corps, killed 7 May 1917'. (Imperial War Museum Q27283)

SE 5a

20ft 11in.

9ft 6in.

26ft 7.4in.

Jasta 11 – in spite of Lothar himself claiming a Sopwith Triplane that day, German eyewitnesses reported seeing Ball's SE 5 emerge from a thick cloud at 200ft, inverted, with its propeller stationary, before crashing. Once his body had been removed from the wreckage, Ball was found to have a broken neck and leg, but no bullet wounds. It is possible that he had become disoriented in the cloud, and while flying inverted the Hispano-Suiza's large float-chambered caburettor flooded the air intake, causing the engine to stall. To top off a melancholy day, 2Lt Roger M. Chaworth-Musters was shot down and killed by Ltn Werner Voss of *Jasta* 'Boelcke'.

In the wake of 7 May's setbacks, Ball's misgivings about the SE 5 re-emerged with a vengeance. B Flight leader Crowe was having none of that, however, for he recognised the scout's positive qualities and its potential. Until successors could be found for Ball and Meintjes, Crowe led all three flights, helping to keep its pilots fighting while simultaneously rebuilding their confidence in their aeroplanes.

The replacement of the SE 5's 150hp Hispano-Suiza with a more powerful 200hp model, along with further refinements, produced the SE 5a, the first of which began arriving at No. 56 Sqn in June 1917. Fast, rugged and almost viceless, the SE 5a became a mainstay of the RFC and later of the RAF over the Western Front right up until the end of the war. The first unit to employ it, 'Fighting Fifty-Six' was also the most successful, being credited with 401 victories by the end of the war and producing numerous famous aces, two of whom – Albert Ball and James Thomas Byford McCudden – were awarded Britain's highest military decoration, the Victoria Cross.

ALBATROS D V

Since the summer of 1915, Germany's first single-seat fighters (Fokker E I, E II and E III) had dominated the airspace over the Western Front. This was not due to their outstanding performance, but because they were armed with a machine gun whose fire was stopped whenever the propeller was in front of it by means of a cam-and-pushrod-operated interruptor gear mechanism. The 'Fokker Scourge' could only go on so long, however, before the Allies found ways to counter it. These ranged from pusher scouts such as the DH 2 to tractor fighters with machine guns mounted above the upper wing to fire over the propeller, such as the Nieuport 11 and 16, or with interruptor gear of their own such as the Sopwith Scout (better known as the 'Pup') and the Nieuport 17 and SPAD VII.

By the time the Battle of the Somme commenced on 1 July 1916, Allied fighters had virtually retaken command of the sky. Maj Wilhelm Siegert, commander of the *Idflieg* (*Inspektion der Fliegertruppen*, or Inspectorate of Aviation Troops), wrote in outspoken retrospect:

The start of the Somme battle unfortunately coincided with the low point in the technical development of our aircraft. The unquestioned supremacy we had enjoyed in early 1916 by virtue of our Fokker monoplane fighters shifted over to the enemy's

Nieuport, Vickers (a German misidentification of the DH 2) and Sopwith aircraft in March and April. Our monthly aircraft output did not even allow a squadron to be equipped with a common type. For example, Fl Abt 23 had a complement of five different aircraft types.

By October 1916, the aerial balance of power began to shift again. In large degree Siegert attributed the German resurgence to the 'enterprise of Boelcke and his "school", in conjunction with the new Halberstadt D II fighter'. That was not exactly true, however. Granted, the Halberstadt biplanes, most notably the D II, proved to be less fragile and had better overall performance than Fokker's *Eindecker* (monoplanes) or the D I, D II, D III and D IV biplanes intended to replace them.

The importance of the Halberstadt D I and D II, however, was more transitionary in nature, both in terms of it establishing the biplane as being more structurally sound than the monoplane and as an early mainstay of the new, specialised fighter squadrons, or *Jagdstaffeln*. The latter began to form in August 1916 starting with *Jasta* 1, organised from Abwehr Kommando Nord under the command of Hptm Martin Zander on the 22nd, followed by *Jasta* 2, under Hptm Oswald Boelcke, on the 27th. Both units started out with Fokker D Is and D IIs, but *Jasta* 2 also received the forerunner of a far more significant line of fighters, the Albatros D I.

Built in the summer of 1916 by the Albatros Werke at Johannesthal, near Berlin, the D I was based on a racing aeroplane developed pre-war by Robert Thelen, supervisor of the Albatros design committee. Its single-bay, twin-spar wing structure was standard for the time, but what distinguished the D I was its streamlined plywood fuselage with a neatly cowled 160hp Mercedes D III engine and a spinner over the propeller. Taking advantage of the more powerful engine, Thelen built the new fighter to carry not one but two synchronised 7.92mm Maxim 08/15 machine guns using Hedtke interruptor gear – a system similar to Fokker's, developed by an Albatros *Werkmeister* – which more than doubled the rate of fire.

The first in a long line of successful fighter scouts, the Albatros D I was derived from a pre-war racing aeroplane. Early examples, such as this machine, were issued to *Jasta* 2 in September 1916. After Lt d R Dieter Collin had scored two victories in this aeroplane with *Jasta* 'Boelcke', it was flown by *Prinz* Friedrich Karl of Prussia, who is seen here fastening his flying helmet in preparation for flight. (Greg VanWyngarden)

Although the Albatros was not as manoeuvrable as most of its Allied opponents, German airmen soon decided that they could live with that, given its superior speed and firepower. They complained more about the way their upward vision was blocked by the upper wing and the trestle-type centre-section struts, to which Thelen quickly responded by lowering the upper wing and supporting it with N-shaped cabane struts splayed outward. He designated the modified scout the Albatros D II. Thelen later replaced the drag-creating 'ear' type Windhoff radiators on the fuselage sides of the D I and early D IIs with a Teeves und Braun radiator installed flush within the upper wing centre section.

One of *Jasta* 2's earliest members, Ltn Erwin Böhme, wrote of the impression the Albatrosen made upon their arrival:

> Their climb rate and manoeuvrability are astonishing – it is as if they are living, feeling beings that understand what their master wishes. With them, one can dare and achieve anything.

Boelcke opened *Jasta* 2's account with seven victories scored in Fokker and Halberstadt scouts. Then, on 16 September, five Albatros D Is and one D II arrived. Flying a D I that same afternoon, Ltn Otto Walter Höhne brought down an FE 2b of No. 11 Sqn at Manacourt, where its crew, 2Lt A. L. Pinkerton and Lt J. W. Sanders, was taken prisoner.

The next morning, Boelcke inaugurated an innovation more significant than the Albatros itself – a systematic team effort focused on gaining local air superiority. Leading five of his men to the frontline, he spotted 14 British aircraft bombing Marcoing railway station. Staying behind and above so that he would be able to come to the aid of any inexperienced pilot who got into trouble, Boelcke sent his charges diving on the enemy formations, which they broke up and then went after individual targets. One of Boelcke's young disciples, Ltn Manfred *Freiherr* von Richthofen, sent an FE 2b crashing at Flesquières aerodrome, killing 2Lts Thomas Rees and Lionel B. F. Morris of No. 11 Sqn. Boelcke and Ltn d R Hans Reimann also downed FE 2bs, while Böhme brought down one of their Sopwith 1½ Strutter escorts of No. 70 Sqn.

The Albatros D II, combined with the adoption of the 'Boelcke Dicta', resulted in another reversal of fortune over the Western Front in the autumn of 1916. *Jasta* 2 headed a general resurgence of German air power, during which Boelcke brought his personal score up to 40 before being killed in a mid-air collision with Böhme (who survived) on 28 October 1916.

By 7 January 1917, *Jasta* 2, renamed *Jasta* 'Boelcke' in its late commander's honour, had been credited with shooting down 87 Allied aircraft in four months – including 16 by von Richthofen, who was awarded the *Orden Pour le Mérite* and given command of *Jasta* 11 at La Brayelle aerodrome. That same day the unit received its first specimen of a new variation on Albatros' winning formula, the D III.

Inspired by the agility and excellent downward visibility afforded by the Nieuport 17, whose single-spar lower wing was little more than an aerofoil-section bracing

These early examples of the fragile Albatros D III were photographed at Proville in the spring of 1917, assigned to *Jasta* 'Boelcke'. The unit's highly capable OzbV (adjutant or special duties officer), Oblt Karl Bodenschatz, is seen kneeling at centre with a *Staffel* mascot named 'Joffre'. Ltn Otto Bernert stands at right, while pilot Ltn Hans Eggers stands at left. Behind Bodenschatz can be seen Ltn d R Hermann Frommherz' pale blue D III, and the nose of Ltn d R 'Fritz' Kempf's Albatros is just visible at extreme right. (*Prien Album*)

structure for the two-spar upper wing (hence the term sesquiplane or '1½-wing'), the Albatros design team tried to achieve the best of both worlds by applying a similar wing arrangement to the D II. The result, which featured two wings with a long curving rake at the tips, the lower of which was of considerably reduced chord, certainly looked more graceful than the squared-off wings of the D II. These in turn provided a superior downward view for the pilot, and gave the D III improved manoeuvrability and a better rate of climb than the D II. *Idflieg* ordered 400 of the new fighters in October 1916, and *Jasta* 24 reported receiving its first three D IIIs on 21 December.

It soon came to light, however, that the improved qualities of the D III came at a price. The Albatros was heavier and more powerful than the Nieuport 17, with its 110hp Le Rhône rotary engine, and German pilots were alarmed to discover that the D III's lower wing would often twist about on its axis during a prolonged dive.

On 17 January 1917, Armee Oberkommando 2 reported four cases of 'rib fractures and breakage of the leading edge' following tight-turning manoeuvres and extended dives. Five days later, whilst diving after a SPAD VII, Ltn Roland Nauck of *Jasta* 6 reported that the lower right wing of his D III had shed its fabric and then the spar itself had broken away, although he managed to land the crippled scout.

On 24 January it was von Richthofen's turn. Soon after taking charge of *Jasta* 11, and while indoctrinating his men in the 'Boelcke Dicta', he had opened the *Staffel's* account in his newly painted all-red D III by shooting down an FE 8 single-seat pusher fighter over Lens on the 23rd, killing 2Lt John Hay of No. 40 Sqn. The following day von Richthofen brought down an FE 2b whose wounded crewmen, Capt Oscar Greig and Lt John E Maclennan of No. 25 Sqn, were taken prisoner. Von Richthofen alighted nearby, but not for a chat. 'One of my wings broke during the air battle at 3,000 metres altitude,' he explained in a letter to his mother a few days later. 'It was only through a miracle that I reached the ground without going *kaput*.'

Von Richthofen's confidence in the new D III was all the more shaken when he learned that *Jasta* 'Boelcke' had reported three similar incidents involving structural failure in the lower wing that very day – one of which killed five-victory ace Off Stv Leopold Reimann. Over the next two months von Richthofen flew an older, but more reliable, Halberstadt D II, which he apparently also painted red, and in which he may have scored as many as 11 victories.

Responding swiftly to the crisis, Albatros strengthened and braced the lower wing cellule sufficiently for the D III to resume operations just in time for the burst of aerial activity that attended Gen Robert Nivelle's spring 1917 offensive. Flown with aggressiveness and tactical skill by von Richthofen and the pilots he inspired, the D III became the terror of the Western Front in a lopsided three-to-one slaughter of British aircraft that came to be known as 'Bloody April'. Satisfied with this success, *Idflieg* ordered more D IIIs, not only from Johannisthal but also from the Ostdeutsche Albatros Werke (OAW) subsidiary in Scheidemühl.

Even while new D III orders were coming in, Albatros spent April further refining its formula. One improvement was the by-product of an experimental D II variant called the D IV, built to test reduction gear that allowed the Mercedes III engine to be repositioned within a fully enclosed cowling, while simultaneously increasing the airscrew's propulsive efficiency. Three D IV airframes were ordered by *Idflieg* in November 1916, but during ground testing airscrew vibration was so bad as to render the aeroplane unflyable. Later tests with three- and four-bladed propellers at least got the scout off the ground, but its lacklustre climb rate (it took a full 32 minutes to reach 5,000ft) and still-unacceptable vibration led to the D IV's abandonment in April 1917.

Although its geared engine was a failure, the D IV successfully introduced a more finely streamlined, elliptical cross-section fuselage than the D II's, along with a more rounded rudder profile and an altered tailskid fairing. Albatros combined these features with the D III's engine layout, which saw much of the cylinder block exposed to the elements. The D III's sesquiplane wing arrangement was also retained, but the gap between the upper and lower flying surfaces was reduced by some 110cm. More significantly, the fuselage-wing joint was less substantial than the D III's and the aileron cables were rerouted through the upper wing, rather than the lower. The

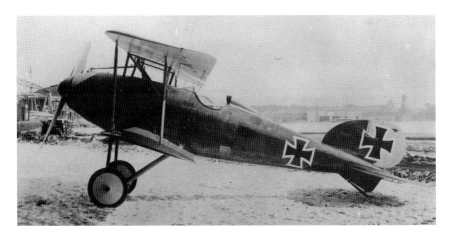

The Albatros D IV's geared engine was a failure, but its fuselage influenced the design of the Albatros D III's successor. Unfortunately for the Germans, its wings did not. (Greg VanWyngarden)

The prototype Albatros D V, still using a D III-type rudder, had its fuselage painted in the same lozenge pattern as the preprinted camouflage fabric on its wings. The D IV's rounder rudder was soon adopted and the headrest abandoned. (Greg VanWyngarden)

OPPOSITE
Albatros D V of Ltn Karl Menckhoff, *Jasta* 3, based at Rumbeke in the autumn of 1917. Born in Herford, Westphalia, on 14 April 1883, Menckhoff served in Infantry Regiment Nr 106 before a wound rendered him unfit for soldiering. Transferring to the air service, he flew in two-seaters over Russia and then served as an instructor, prior to joining *Jasta* 3 in early 1917. First scoring on 5 April, Menckhoff had raised his total to 20 – including three SE 5as – and earned a commission by 11 February 1918, when he was given command of *Jasta* 72s. With this unit he downed 19 more aeroplanes and had been awarded the *Orden Pour le Mérite* by 25 July 1918, when, much to his embarrassment, he was brought down by the relatively inexperienced American SPAD XIII pilot 1Lt Walter L. Avery of the 95th Aero Squadron. Later escaping from a French PoW camp to Switzerland, Menckhoff settled there post-war, and had become a successful businessman by the time of his death in 1948.

resultant 'lightened Albatros D III airframe', designated the D V, weighed 50kg less than the D III.

Strangely, considering its previous D III experience, *Idflieg's* engineers tested the new aeroplane's fuselage and rudder but failed to static-test the wings before ordering 200 D Vs. The first examples began arriving at the front in May, and almost from the outset reports came in of wingtip flutter and structural failure. The lightened fuselage structure also proved to be prone to cracking during rough landings, resulting in the aircraft literally breaking up. Within the month *Idflieg* was doing belated stress testing, and concluding, to its dismay, that the D V's sesquiplane wing layout was even more vulnerable than that of its predecessor. To make matters worse, the new scout's performance was much the same as the D III. An urgent call for better fighters was issued, including a triplane, inspired (much as the Albatros sesquiplanes had been inspired by the Nieuports) by the remarkably agile Sopwith Triplane.

Circumstances conspired against the complete abandonment of the Albatros D V, however. On 6 April 1917, the United States declared war on Germany, and recognition of the industrial potential of its new adversary led to a drastic expansion of German air power on 23 June. Among other things, the so-called *Amerikaprogramm* called for the formation of 40 new *Jagdstaffeln* and a second *Jastaschule* to help train the new fighter pilots selected from 24,000 recruits.

Pending the appearance of a suitable Albatros D V replacement in the face of the American threat, *Idflieg* saw no alternative to placing production orders for more D Vs – 400 in May and 300 in July. In a letter to his friend Oblt Fritz von Falkenhayn on the *Luftstreitskäfte* staff on 18 July 1917, von Richthofen complained of the inadequate quality, as well as numbers, of the aircraft he now led against the Allies over the Flanders front:

The D V is so obsolete and so ridiculously inferior to the English that one can't do anything with this aircraft. But the people at home have not bought anything new for almost a year, except for this lousy Albatros, and we have remained stuck with the D III.

Nevertheless, as of 31 August, Albatros products – 424 D Vs, 385 D IIIs and 56 D IIs and D Is – made up 84 percent of the 1,030 fighters in the frontline inventory.

ALBATROS D V

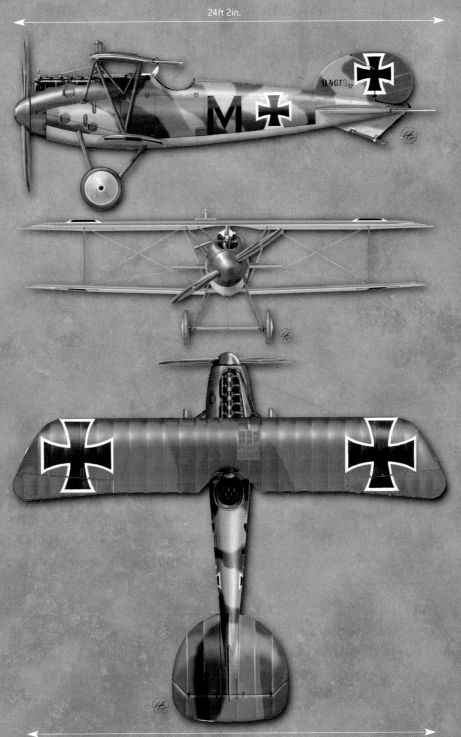

24ft 2in.

8ft 10.25in.

29ft 6in.

This consignment of early-build Albatros D Vs that was delivered to *Jasta* 11 included D.1166/17 and D.1177/17, both of which were later flown by Rittm Manfred *Freiherr* von Richthofen. (Greg VanWyngarden)

In August 1917 the Pfalz D III and Fokker F I made their debuts at the front. The Pfalz, a true biplane whose two-spar lower wing had less area than the upper, was sturdier than the Albatros, but pilots complained of sluggish performance indicative of an inferior power-to-weight ratio. Fokker's pre-production F I was a triplane with an advanced cantilever wing structure. Although boasting a spectacular rate of climb and outstanding manoeuvrability, its production variant, the Dr I, suffered structural failures in late October and early November 1917 that were traced to poor quality control. The triplane's arrival in force was delayed while Fokker rectified the situation. In the meantime, most German fighter pilots would have to make do with the Albatros D V.

Hptm Kurt von Döring, *Staffelführer* of *Jasta* 4, walks mascots 'Vickers', 'SPAD' and 'Nieuport' down a line-up of new Albatros D Vs marked with the unit's black fuselage ribbon, as well as individually coloured spinners and tails. (Charles Donald Collection via Jon Guttman)

TECHNICAL SPECIFICATIONS

SE 5

For a total production run of just 77, counting the two prototypes, the SE 5 came in an unusual number of incarnations – all necessary, as it turned out, for its eventual success as the SE 5a. The second production batch, starting with A8898, featured wings of reduced span, which improved lateral handling characteristics. A comparison of performance might be derived from the following statistics for A4845 in its original configuration and the modified, lightened, reduced wingspan A8911.

SE 5a

Even while No. 56 Sqn was slowly breaking in its SE 5s in France, the Royal Aircraft Factory was developing the most significant improvement in the aeroplane by mounting Hispano-Suiza's new, geared-down, 200hp 8B engine in the third SE 5 prototype, A4563. Using a four-bladed propeller, but retaining the SE 5's original L-shaped exhaust manifolds, A4563 also had the less-raked, shorter-span wings that would be a feature of the SE 5a.

During its first test flight at Martlesham Heath, in Suffolk, on 29 May, the aircraft displayed improved lateral control, as well as a top speed of 123mph at 14,000ft. This compared favourably with the SE 5's maximum of 105mph at 15,000ft. The climb rate was also improved, with A4863 reaching 14,000ft in 16 minutes, compared to

	SE 5 A4845	SE 5 A8911
Engine	Aries Hispano-Suiza	Wolseley Hispano-Suiza
Wingspan	27ft 11in	26ft 7.4in
Wing area	249.8 sq. ft	244 sq. ft
Chord	5ft	5ft
Dihedral	five degrees	five degrees
Length	20ft 11in	20ft 11in
Height	9ft 5in	9ft 5in
Armament	one 0.303-in. Vickers	one 0.303-in. Vickers
	one 0.303-in. Lewis	one 0.303-in. Lewis
Weight (lb)		
Empty	1,399	-
Loaded	1,930	1,892
Max speed (mph)		
At 6,500ft	119	120
At 10,000ft	114	116
At 15,000ft	98	105

Climb to	minutes	seconds	minutes	seconds
5,000ft	5	36	-	-
6,500ft	8	0	7	50
10,000ft	14	15	13	42
15,000ft	29	30	28	12
Service Ceiling (feet)	17,000		16,500	
Endurance (hours)	2½		2½	

The cockpit of a preserved SE 5a at the Australian War Memorial Museum in Canberra reveals the serious attempt made by the Royal Aircraft Factory to organise a functional instrument panel within the scout. (Steve St Martin Collection via Jon Guttman)

the 27 minutes it took an SE 5 to reach 15,000ft. Before even getting official approval – although it was certainly forthcoming – the Royal Aircraft Factory fitted 15 SE 5s of the second production batch with the 200hp Hispano-Suizas and shipped A8923 to No. 56 Sqn on 8 June, followed by A4563 three days later.

Assigned to B Flight and marked up as 'B6', A4563 had a fairly long and productive career that saw 2Lt Arthur P F Rhys Davids score at least eight victories in it by 7 September, after which the scout was passed on to 2Lt Verschoyle P. Cronyn. The latter flew it in No. 56 Sqn's famous 23 September 1917 melee with 48-victory ace Ltn Werner Voss, who shot it up badly enough for A4563 to be written off. Cronyn survived, shaken, but miraculously unhurt.

Meanwhile, the Royal Aircraft Factory refined the new SE 5a, fixing problems with the Hispano-Suiza's carburettor and adopting long

SE 5a COCKPIT

1. Radiator shutter control lever
2. Mixture control lever
3. Throttle lever
4. Transfer air selector switch and valve
5. Fuel air transfer pressure gauge
6. Fuel selector switch
7. 0.303-in Vickers machine gun
8. Gun mounting bracket
9. Fuel gauge
10. Windscreen
11. Detachable auxiliary instrument panel
12. Airspeed indicator (knots)
13. Accelerometer
14. Altimeter
15. Oil temperature gauge
16. Oil pressure gauge
17. RPM indicator
18. Airspeed indicator (mph)
19. Radiator temperature gauge
20. Altimeter
21. Compass
22. Gun triggers
23. Slip bubble
24. Control column grip
25. Control column
26. Rudder pedals
27. Tailplane incidence control
28. Priming pump
29. Gunsight
30. Magneto switch
31. Magneto switch
32. Seat
33. Bomb release lever
34. Vickers gun ammunition feed
35. Clock

exhaust pipes similar to the SPAD VII pipes Albert Ball had had 'custom installed' on his SE 5 A4850 – these became standard for all SE 5s and SE 5as from 10 July onward.

In addition to the Royal Aircraft Factory, seven other subcontractors built the SE 5a under license, including Austin, Martinsyde, Vickers and Wolseley.

The RFC had ordered 3,600 SE 5as by the end of 1917, and while more than 800 airframes were built by 29 December, some 400 of these lay idle in storage awaiting the fitment of engines. Only Wolseley Motors Ltd held a license to build Hispano-Suiza 8Bs, and its products were proving to be chronically defective. While France placed the highest priority on supplying engines for its own new SPAD XIIIs, some Hispano-Suiza engines found their way into SE 5as as well. A small number of the latter machines were also fitted with Brasier-built 8Bs, but their reduction gears and airscrew shafts were so unreliable that they had to be replaced with British spares. The engine problem had reached crisis proportions by January 1918, when the Air Board managed to get its hands on the first of 8,000 Hispano-Suizas it had ordered from French contractors.

Four months earlier, a misinterpretation of a desperate order for an additional 400 direct-drive 150hp Hispano-Suizas led Wolseley to a serendipitous development. The company increased the compression ratio from 4.68 to 5.3 and duly got the engine to reliably produce 200hp at 2,000rpm. The first ten examples of the new engine, designated the W 4A Viper, were built at the end of August 1917. After testing at Martlesham, the Viper proved to be so much better (it increased the fighter's top speed by a full 7mph and improved its rate of climb) than the Wolesley-built geared Hispano-Suiza that it was approved for full production. In order to accommodate the new engine, Wolseley modified the SE 5a so that it had a lower thrust line for the shaft, which in turn drove a two-bladed propeller once again. The scout also boasted a squarer radiator with two sets of horizontal shutters.

SE 5a B4897 featured a strengthened undercarriage when inspected at the Farnborough air depot on 17–20 November 1917. Ferried to No. 60 Sqn on the 26th, it was on an OP on 24 January 1918 when it collided with an Albatros over Beceleare at 1210 hrs. Both pilots, Lt A. W. Morey and Ltn d R Martin Möbius of *Jasta 7*, were killed. (Greg VanWyngarden)

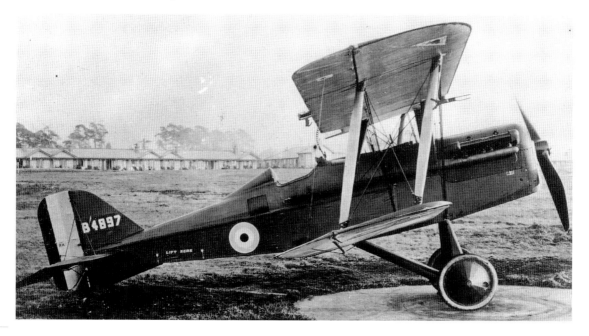

Another alternative engine considered for the SE 5a was the Sunbeam Arab. The geared Arab I was tested in November 1917 and the direct-drive Arab II two months later. Although this effort proceeded through to the spring of 1919, vibration problems rendered both engines unsatisfactory.

The fighter also benefited from the continued evolution of the Constantinesco-Colley CC hydraulic interruptor gear, whose mechanical parts were now kept lubricated by a paraffin-oil mix, rather than simply by oil alone. This in turn gave the SE 5a a Vickers gun that was less prone to failure, and whose rate of fire was less dependent upon the speed of the engine, whether throttled up or down, when compared with other mechanical systems used by its Allied and German contemporaries. This was particularly welcome on those SE 5as with four-bladed propellers, which would

A demonstration of the overwing Foster mount for the SE 5a's Lewis machine gun. A few aces – most notably Albert Ball and Jimmy McCudden – used it for attacking the undersides of enemy aircraft. Others extended the Lewis gun handle to facilitate pulling it down to change drums. (Jon Guttman)

Some SE 5a pilots put bulged panels on the cockpit sides to give themselves more elbow room. In the case of No. 32 Sqn, whose scouts are shown here ready for take-off from Pronville on 6 April 1918, they cut away part of the cockpit coaming to improve the pilot's shoulder room. Serials and flight markings have been crudely blotted out of this photograph by the wartime censor. (Greg VanWyngarden)

SE 5a Dimensions

Engine	200hp Hispano-Suiza 8B
Wingspan	26ft 7.4in
Wing area	245.8 sq. ft
Chord	5ft
Dihedral	five degrees
Length	20ft 11in
Height	9ft 6in
Armament	one 0.303-in Vickers
	one 0.303-in Lewis
	four 25lb Cooper bombs
Weight (lb)	
Empty	1,531
Loaded	2,048
Maximum speed (mph)	
10,000 ft	126
15,000 ft	116.5

Climb to	minutes	seconds
10,000ft	13	15
15,000ft	27	35
Service Ceiling (feet)	17,000	
Endurance (hours)	2½	

otherwise have been handicapped by a truly damaging effect on their rate of fire compared to that of SE 5as using two-bladed airscrews.

Further modifications were made on SE 5as, both at home and operationally. The landing gear was strengthened further, and most squadrons also added an additional bracing wire to the leading edge of the fin. Some SE 5as, including Capt James T. B. McCudden's B4891 of No. 56 Sqn, had ailerons and elevators of reduced chord. A number of pilots in No. 24 Sqn also reduced the scout's wing dihedral for better manoeuvrability, and many removed the headrest to improve the rearward view. Some SE 5s and SE 5as were modified with bulged fairings on the cockpit sides, while a number of scouts assigned to No. 32 Sqn featured a cut-out space in the after part of the cockpit.

By the end of World War I, 2,765 SE 5/5as had been built, and some 2,500 more would be completed before production ceased in 1919. Not only did the SE 5/5a prove to be more than a match for the Albatros D V in 1917, but the Viper-engined SE 5a would hold its own against the more advanced Fokker D VII a year later.

ALBATROS D V

As the data on page 31 reveals, Albatros' 'lightened' airframe D V had an inferior rate of climb when compared with the 'heavy' D III. And it was structurally suspect too.

The response from within the *Jagdstaffeln* upon receiving the D V swiftly changed from hopeful enthusiasm to alarm, and then resignation, as pilots made the best of a

Albatros D Vs of *Jasta* 22 at Vivaise aerodrome in the summer of 1917. Although the D V looked racier than the D III when it first appeared in late April 1917, disappointment soon set in. (Jon Guttman)

Albatros	D III		D V (original)	
Engine	160hp Mercedes D III		160hp Mercedes D III	
Wingspan (upper)	29ft 6in		29ft 6in	
(lower)	28ft 10in		28ft 8in	
Wing area	225 sq. ft		224 sq. ft	
Chord (upper wing)	4ft 11in		4ft 11in	
(lower wing)	3ft 4in		3ft 4in	
Dihedral	two degrees (lower wing only)		two degrees (lower wing only)	
Length	24ft ½in		24ft 2in	
Height	9ft 6in		8ft 10¼in	
Armament	two 7.92mm LMG 08/15s		two 7.92mm LMG 08/15s	
Weight (lb)				
Empty	1,481		1,368	
Useful load	518		518	
Loaded	1,999		1,874	
Maximum speed (mph)	108.73		116	
Climb to	minutes	seconds	minutes	seconds
3,050ft	2	30	4	20
6,100ft	6	0	8	50
9,150ft	11	0	14	30
12,200ft	17	0	22	40
15,250ft	24	30	35	0

disappointing job. Ground crews as well as the Albatros *Werke* itself took steps to reinforce the fighter's fragile wing structures, usually with extra bracing wires or a small auxiliary strut from the lower front of the V-shaped interplane strut to the lower wing. Early D Vs were delivered with large headrests, which nearly all the pilots – like a good many of their SE 5-flying opponents – regarded as nothing but an impediment to their rearward view, so they had them removed. The second production batch of D Vs and subsequent D Vas dispensed with the headrests entirely.

Other than these measures, little more was done on operational Albatros D Vs. The most significant changes occurred with the development of the D Va.

ALBATROS D Va

In August 1917 Albatros, although still unable to ascertain the cause of the D V's wing failures, sought an interim remedy by giving it stronger wing spars (wrapped in aluminium for extra flexibility), heavier ribs, additional wing support cables and,

An Albatros D Va of *Jasta* 50 shows the added cables, auxiliary interplane strut brace and aileron cable rerouted from the lower to the upper wing as per the D III – as well as a reinforced fuselage that nevertheless failed to stand up to the violence associated with this particular crash-landing. (Jon Guttman)

sometimes, a small auxiliary bracing strut at the base of the interplane strut. This was largely a standardisation of improvised or retroactive measures already seen on the D V, but in addition the aileron cables were rerouted through the lower wings, as they had been on the D III, and the fuselage structure was reinforced using an appreciably thicker gauge of plywood. Also introduced in August was an improved interruptor gear for the machine guns, devised for Albatros by a *Werkmeister* Semmler, to replace the Hedtke gear.

Satisfied with these modifications, in spite of the fact that the airframe was now heavier than that of the D III, let alone the D V, *Idflieg* placed an order for the first of an eventual 1,600 Albatros D Vas in August 1917, even though it did not complete its tests of the new type until December. That, and the placing of a last D III order with OAW as late as September 1917, reflected the *Luftstreitskräfte's* desperation as it tried to build itself up for the expected arrival of the US Army Air Service in early 1918, even while its *Jagdflieger* strove to counter a series of Allied offensives in the summer and autumn of 1917.

There was virtually no difference between the Albatros D V and D Va dimensionally, but the latter's strengthened airframe resulted in an unwelcome loaded weight increase from 1,886lb to 1,953lb. Initially, the D Va's performance suffered, but in early 1918 Mercedes produced the D IIIa engine – essentially the D III with a higher compression ratio and later re-engineered with oversize cylinders and pistons. The result was an increase in output from 170hp to 185hp. Various sub-variants of this engine were

A superb cockpit interior view of an Albatros D Va of *Jasta* 75 at Habsheim aerodrome in the summer of 1918. Note the signal gun outside the cockpit at right and ample clips of extra flares within the pilot's reach on both sides of the fuselage. (Greg VanWyngarden)

subsequently produced, such as the D IIIaü and D IIIaüv, the latter weighing 33lb more than the former. Being the main powerplant used in the OAW-built D Va, it helped raise the aeroplane's empty weight to 1,496lb.

At best, all the improved Mercedes motor could do was restore the D Va's performance to that of its lighter, but more fragile, predecessor, the maximum speed, for example, topping out at 116.81mph. All the same, in light of the coming spring offensive, and the paucity of better fighters pending the arrival in quantity of the Fokker D VII, the development of the Mercedes D IIIa could not have come at a more critical juncture for the German army and naval air services. Indeed, this engine was also fitted to the D Va's supplementary stablemate, the Pfalz D IIIa.

Concurrent with the introduction of the Albatros D V was a gradual change in the camouflage on its wings and tail surfaces, from painted-on patches of dark green and mauve to directly applied fabric panels in lozenges of four or five varying shades, dark for the upper surfaces and lighter for the lower. These were supposed to achieve an overall camouflage effect when viewed at a distance, although that was often rendered moot by the frequent practice of decorating the aircraft in flamboyant *Staffel* colours and personal motifs! Perhaps more importantly, the preprinted fabric saved the weight that painting added, needing only an application of protective clear dope.

Two interesting experiments involved D Va airframes. Amid *Idflieg's* general clamour for a worthy counterpart to the Sopwith Triplane, Albatros stacked three identical short-chord wings with flush radiators on the middle pair and three sets of ailerons on a D Va fuselage to produce the Dr I. Tests revealed the aeroplane to be tail-heavy, apt to fall into spins and more obstructive to the pilot's vision than the sesquiplane, while offering no worthwhile improvement in performance. Hence, like nearly all other German triplane prototypes, Albatros' fell by the wayside.

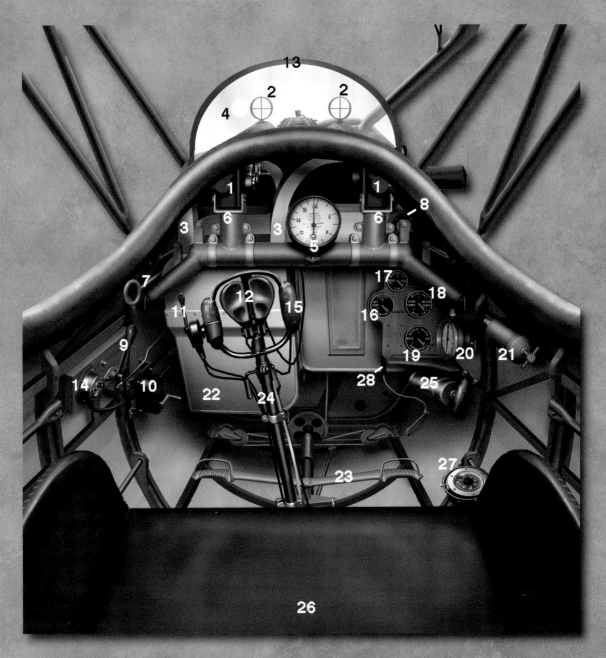

1. 7.92mm LMG 08/15 machine guns
2. Ring and bead sights
3. Ammunition chutes
4. Windscreen with hole at left to allow vision if stained with oil
5. Tachometer
6. Machine gun mounting brackets
7. Auxiliary throttle handle
8. Fuel pressure gauge
9. Spark control handle
10. Starting magneto
11. Throttle handle
12. Machine gun buttons
13. Windscreen
14. Magneto switch key
15. Control column grip
16. Air pressure selector handle
17. Fuel pressure gauge
18. Air pump selector gauge
19. Air pressure gauge
20. Fuel quantity gauge
21. Water pump greaser
22. Ammunition belt container in front of two ammunition cans
23. Rudder control bar
24. Control column
25. Hand-operated air pump
26. Adjustable leather-padded aluminium seat
27. Magnetic compass
28. Drain cock

Oblt Eduard *Ritter* von Schleich, commander of *Jagdgruppe* 8, sits in the cockpit of his black Albatros D Va, accessorised with a flare rack and Oigee tube gunsight. (Greg VanWyngarden)

In February 1918, an *Ingenieur* Kändler from the Siemens-Schuckert Werke visited *Jasta* 5's aerodrome at Boistrancourt with two D Vas equipped with a pair of motor machine guns developed by his firm, touted as capable of firing 1,400 rounds per minute. Bearing stylised bones on the fuselage sides – and one also sporting black and white spiral stripes – they were photographed on 25 February behind Kändler, a bevy of mechanics and the two aces for whom they were evidently intended, Vfws Josef Mai and Fritz Rumey. The latter shot down a DH 4 north of Busigny the next day for his ninth victory, but it remains undetermined whether he did so using the new weapons. In any case, such armament was not adopted for production, probably because of its complexity and the consequent maintenance problems that were anticipated.

Two Albatros D Vas experimentally fitted with Siemens-Schuckert motor machine guns capable of firing 1,400 rounds per minute arrived at *Jasta* 5's Boistrancourt aerodrome on 25 February 1918. Off Stv Josef Mai is standing third from left, beside *Ingenieur* Kaendler of SSW, while Vfw Fritz Rumey leans on the other aeroplane's wing. Mai's moon-marked D Va 5284/17 can just be seen in the left background. Rumey may have used the aeroplane at right to shoot down a DH 4 over Busigny the day after this photograph was taken. (Johan Visser via Jon Guttman)

The stripped wrecks of several Oeffag-built Albatros D IIIs (and a lone Phönix D I, parked third from left) are seen here lined up by the Italians on Bressanone airfield on a cold November 1918 day. (Paolo Variale)

An ironic sidebar to the Albatros story concerns the Oeffag-Albatros D III, a license-built version produced by the Oesterreichische Flugzeugbau AG in Weiner-Neustadt for the Austro-Hungarian air service. Built using superior wood by skilled craftsmen, the Oeffags held up well in combat, even while using larger, heavier but more powerful Austro-Daimler engines of 185hp, 200hp and finally 225hp, the latter endowing the Series 253 D III with a maximum speed of 125mph and the ability to climb to 15,250ft in 20 minutes and 5 seconds.

Although the Oeffag's construction seems to have alleviated, if not eliminated, the sesquiplane curse, pilot complaints of spinners coming off in flight led to them being done away with on late production series 153 and all 253 series D IIIs, which mounted the propeller in front of a rounded nose cowl with no adverse effect on the fighter's performance.

Austro-Hungarian pilots regarded the Oeffag 253 series D III as their best fighter, superior to the indigenously produced Phönix D II and Berg D I. Equally significant, however, are the production figures of these excellent machines – at least 203 Series 253s were built out of a grand total of about 550 Oeffag D IIIs of all series. In comparison, Albatros produced about 900 D Vs and 1,012 D Vas, to which OAW added another 600 D Vas. Austria-Hungary offered superior quality with its Oeffag-built Albatrosen, but at what proved to be a fatal sacrifice in quantity.

STRATEGIC
SITUATION

THE SOMME AND FLANDERS IN 1917

The failure of Gen Erich von Falkenhayn's war of attrition at Verdun, the British Somme Offensive in July 1916 and the stunning success of Russian Gen Aleksei Brusilov's offensive of 4 June–7 July 1916 led to Falkenhayn's replacement as Chief of the General Staff on 29 August 1916 by Paul Ludwig Hans Anton von Beneckendorff und von Hindenburg. The latter's victories on the Russian Front, especially at Tannenberg in September 1914, had made him a national hero.

With his chief of staff General Erich Ludendorff, the veteran Hindenburg devised a strategy for 1917 based on a defensive stance on the Western Front, while striving for a decisive victory over Russia, which in spite of Brusilov's success was showing signs of political, economic and moral strain that made its collapse an inviting possibility.

Between 21 February and the end of March 1917, the Germans carried out Operation *Alberich* – a general withdrawal across France to a shorter frontline, with well-prepared defences in depth running from Arras along the river Scarpe to the Chemin des Dames ridge. Collectively dubbed the *Siegfried Stellung*, this new position was often referred to by the Allies as the Hindenburg Line.

The German army's defensive posture was reflected in the conduct of the new *Jagdstaffeln* that guarded the airspace over these fortified trench lines and strong points. Given Germany's limited resources, including fuel, and the Allies' overall numerical preponderance in manpower, such a policy made sense. With Allied aircraft venturing over their lines, the Germans could despatch their fighters a shorter distance to wherever they were needed, and enjoy the advantage of a usually westerly wind hindering the Allied aeroplanes' ability to regain their own lines. As Manfred von

Modest gains near Cambrai, largely cancelled out by a German counterattack on 30 November 1917, brought the Passchendaele offensive to an unsatisfactory end for the British. In spite of the Albatros D V's inherent weaknesses, German resistance had been as effective in the air as on the ground throughout the fighting.

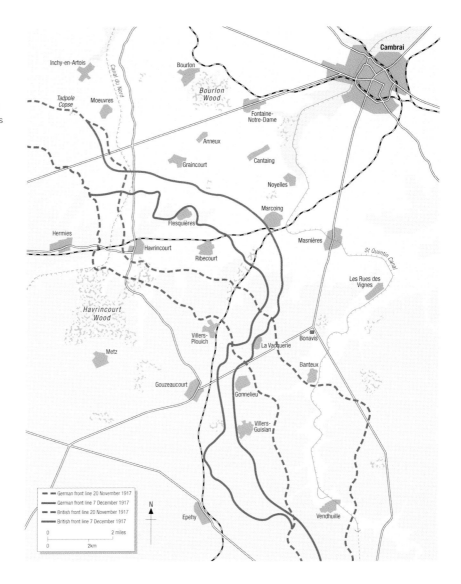

Richthofen related of this period, 'if the enemy insisted on coming to one's shop, why go out looking for customers?'

Even while the Germans reorganised their defensive line, the new French commander-in-chief, General Robert Nivelle, planned a grand, artillery-supported, offensive north along the river Aisne in conjunction with assaults by the British First and Third armies eastward from Arras. The latter were launched in April 1917, and as had been the case during the Battle of the Somme in 1916, Gen Trenchard employed the RFC as aggressively as the Germans husbanded their aerial resources sparingly, launching his fighter squadrons on regular OPs either for a specific purpose (as the French did) or simply to, as he put it, 'reduce the Hun to a proper state of mind'.

Given the superior Albatros D IIIs and tactical advantages possessed by the *Jagdstaffeln* early in 1917, Trenchard's policy played into the enemy's hands, resulting in the three-to-one losses the British suffered during 'Bloody April'. Even amid that

aerial slaughter, however, the RNAS gave the Germans cause for concern with its Sopwith Triplane, while the RFC introduced the SE 5 and the Bristol F 2A Fighter. Although neither of the latter types made a significant impression on the Germans at the time, their more powerful descendants – the SE 5a and the F 2B – soon would.

Also of concern to the Germans was the United States' declaration of war on 6 April, bringing the self-proclaimed birthplace of the aeroplane and an industrial power of vast potential into the conflict. While the German aviation industry strove to create a fighter of equal or superior quality to the new Allied entries, the *Luftstreitskräfte* also had to take quantity into consideration. One consequence was the launching on 23 June of the *Amerikaprogramm*, which doubled the available units – on paper at least.

Another consequence was the need to continue building fighters of a proven design until production of its successor reached full tempo. That proven design was the Albatros D III and its 'lightened' offspring, the D V. Even when the latter was found not to be the significant improvement that its pilots had hoped it would be, for at least six months the *Kommandierte General der Luftstreitskräfte* (*Kogenluft*) could not afford to interfere with production, save for the development of the sturdier, but basically similar, D Va, and German airmen had to do their best with them.

The Nivelle Offensive ended on 20 April with 187,000 French casualties for negligible gains. The British Expeditionary Force (BEF) had suffered 158,660 casualties when the advance from Arras ceased on 17 May. With the French army exhausted and plagued by mutinies, the BEF tried to keep up the pressure by overrunning the salient around Messines Ridge between 7 and 14 June. After that, the *Luftstreitskräfte* finally began doing what the French had already done with their *Groupes de Combat* and the British with their wings – gather and coordinate their *Jasta* operations. Commenting on this pivotal organisational change, Manfred von Richthofen declared:

> During a defensive battle it is best that each *Gruppe* (army group) is assigned a *Jagdgruppe*. This *Jagdgruppe* is not bound strictly to the *Gruppe* sector, but its main purpose is to enable the working aircrews to perform their function and, in exceptional cases, to provide them with immediate protection.

SE 5 A8918 of No. 60 Sqn was being flown by 2Lt H. T. Hammond, from Sydney, New South Wales, when it was brought down by ground fire on 14 September 1917. Hammond was immediately captured, and his near-intact scout thoroughly examined by the Germans. (Greg VanWyngarden)

The *Jasta* 5 line-up at Boistrancourt in late July 1917, as shown on page 6, seen from the opposite end. The third Albatros D V from the right was 2065/17, flown by the CO, Oblt Richard Flashar, whilst the one to the left of it sports the chequered after fuselage and demon's head that identified Vfw Frtiz Rumey at the time. (Greg VanWyngarden)

Moreover, the AOK (*Armee Oberkommando*) has at its disposal a large number of *Jagdstaffeln* (*Geschwadern*), which by all means must be allowed to hunt freely, and whose mission throughout is dedicated to stopping the enemy's flight operations. These AOK forces should not be dispersed for protection flights, escort flights or defensive patrols. Their mission is determined by the *Geschwader Kommandeur* according to the instructions of the *KoFl* (*Kommandeur der Flieger*).

While local units were coordinated as *Jagdgruppen*, their makeup varying according to the situation, von Richthofen commanded the first of the more permanent and mobile *Jagdgeschwader* on 24 June, when *Jastas* 4, 6, 10 and his own 11 were officially combined into JG I. That formation was soon travelling to Flanders, where the British opened a new offensive on 31 July, initiating the agonising 'slugfest' known both as the Third Battle of Ypres and Passchendaele. While fighting on the ground dragged on until 6 November, JG I's tendency to motor from one hot spot to another, the colourful *Staffel* and individual markings on its aeroplanes and the star quality of its pilots combined to earn it the sobriquet of the 'Flying Circus'.

A final British push toward Cambrai, involving the first massed use of tanks, was launched on 20 November. After encouraging initial gains it bogged down, and on the 30th German counterattacks stabilised the front.

By the end of 1917 things were looking up for the Central Powers. Rumania, which had entered the war on the Allied side on 27 August 1916, had been practically neutralised by January 1917, with most of its southern regions occupied – including Ploesti, from which the Germans had appropriated a million tons of vitally needed oil by the end of the war. The Italians were routed by the Austro-Hungarians at Caporetto on 25 October and the concurrent Russian Revolution would lead to Bolshevik capitulation on 3 March 1918, freeing up thousands of German soldiers for service on the Western Front. Only in the Middle East was the news bad, as the British advanced steadily in both Palestine and Mesopotamia.

To Hindenburg and Ludendorff, the time was as ripe as it ever would be to force the French and British into suing for a favourable peace – and with the American Expeditionary Force arriving, it would never be riper.

For the breakthrough offensive, dubbed *Kaiserschlacht*, the Germans massed their aerial as well as ground assets, with three *Jagdgeschwader*, each formed around four *Jastas* by mid-February 1918, to augment the more flexible *Jagdgruppen* in establishing local air superiority over three different army groupings. JG I, at Awoingt, was assigned to the 2. *Armee*. To support the 18. *Armee*, JG II, with *Jastas* 12, 13, 15 and 19, was formed on 2 February under Hptm Adolf *Ritter* von Tutschek, but when he was killed in action on 15 March, the unit came under the command of Hptm Rudolf Berthold and moved to Guise on the 19th. JG III, also formed on 2 February under Oblt Bruno Loerzer and consisting of *Jastas* 'Boelcke', 26, 27 and 36, operated from Erchin to support the 17. *Armee*.

All three *Geschwader* were primarily equipped with the Fokker Dr I, then regarded as the best German fighter available. Von Richthofen and Berthold, however, were already aware of the triplane's limitations – it was slow, and its rotary engine, never a German forte, was chronically unreliable. Promising fighters were in the offing, such as the Fokker D VII and Siemens-Schuckert Werke's SSW D III, but for the time being von Richthofen hedged his bets by fully equipping *Jastas* 6 and 11 with Dr Is, while retaining Albatros D Vas and Pfalz D IIIas in *Jastas* 4 and 10.

Likewise, Berthold's *Jastas* 12, 13 and 19 had triplanes, but *Jasta* 15 flew Albatros D Vas. Loerzer intended all four of JG III's *Staffeln* to use Dr Is, but in February there were only enough Fokkers to supply *Jastas* 'Boelcke' and 36. *Jastas* 26 and 27 continued flying Albatros D Vs well into March. Except for Dr I-equipped *Jasta* 14, the Albatros D Va remained the mainstay of the other *Jagdstaffeln*, with Pfalz D IIIas helping fill out the ranks of the *Amerikaprogramm* units.

As of early March 1918, the German 2., 17. and 18. *Armees* had amassed 730 aeroplanes, 326 of which were fighters, against the British Third and Fifth Armies, which then had 579 operational aircraft, of which 261 were single-seat fighters, in 32 squadrons.

By then SE 5a-equipped Nos 56, 60 and 84 Sqns had been joined by No. 40 Sqn, which had replaced its Nieuports with them, and Nos 24, 32 and 41 Sqns, which

Ltn Hermann Leptien, commander of *Jasta* 63, stands in the middle of his flying officers in March 1918. Typifying the hastily organised *Amerikaprogramm*, *Jasta* 63 was understrength, led by an experienced man (Leptien scored seven victories) and equipped with Albatros D Vas, in this case with black diamonds alternating over the varnished fuselage. (US Air Force Museum via Jon Guttman)

Reflecting 1917's generally defensive stance, German aerodromes along the Western Front were arranged to allow a quick response to British incursions, while simultaneously husbanding their limited resources and making the most of their Albatros D Vs' modest strengths. This tactic enjoyed remarkable success.

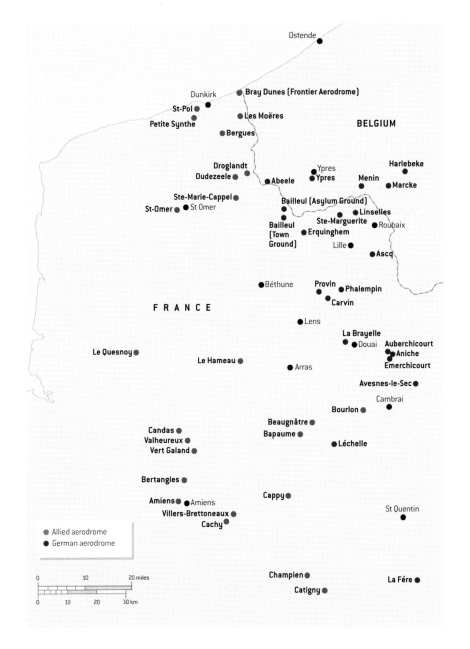

were in the process of replacing their DH 5s with SE 5as. Another DH 5 unit, No. 68 Sqn, was not only acquiring SE 5as but also a new designation as No. 2 Sqn Australian Flying Corps. In addition, Nos 1, 64 and 74 Sqns were working up with SE 5as in England and would soon be making their way to France.

For the time being, though, by mid-March there were eight combat-ready SE 5a units on the Western Front whose theoretical full complements of 18 scouts each totalled – on paper at least – 144 aeroplanes in all sectors of the Western Front. For comparison, at the same time the RFC and RNAS were also fielding no fewer than 336 Camels in 14 squadrons.

THE COMBATANTS

ROYAL FLYING CORPS

One pilot who undertook his flying training just as the SE 5a was reaching operational squadrons in serious quantities was Lt Walter Campbell Daniel, a Canadian who said that he was 'tested, examined, prodded and clothed in service issue uniform with a white band on the forage cap to designate cadet status' on 1 May 1917. After much drilling and instruction, he made his first flights in Curtiss JN 4s at Long Branch field, west of Toronto, and was then shipped out for England aboard the steamship *Metagama* in August.

Once at Tern Hill, in Shropshire, Daniel did his advanced training in the Avro 504K, the Sopwith Pup, which he called 'the greatest pleasure to date' and, finally, the DH 5. From there he undertook a basic gunnery course at Turnberry, in Ayrshire, after which he briefly returned to Tern Hill, prior to being sent to No. 64 Sqn at Izel-le-Hameau.

'Arriving on 21 November 1917, I found that the squadron had been in the midst of the British attack toward Cambrai, which had commenced the day before', Daniel recalled post-war. No. 64 Sqn's DH 5s, poor fighters above 10,000ft, had been primarily used for trench strafing and close support, supplementing their single Vickers machine guns with racks for four 20lb Cooper bombs. Assigned to B Flight under Capt Roland St Clair McClintock, Daniel joined in low-level attack missions on 22, 23 and 24 November.

'On the third day of action, we sent out 18 aeroplanes in the morning. There were only a half-dozen pilots at dinner in the mess, the rest having been widely scattered.'

In the initial offensive, both tanks and infantry penetrated to villages some five miles east of Bourlon Wood, and a gap of several miles width was torn in the

43

German defences. At the end of the month, however, the Germans counterattacked, and by 7 December the Western Front had once again fallen into bloody stalemate. Daniel continued:

> The dull months of January and February were only lightened by the exchange of our DH 5s for SE 5as. We were equipped with the oldest extant models of SE 5a early in 1918, and the change from a rotary-powered machine with the character of the DH 5 to the SE 5a was pretty drastic. They gave us better aeroplanes later on.
>
> The SE 5a, with its heavier nose and Hispano-Suiza liquid-cooled engine was more stable than the DH 5 or the Camel, but it required some time for familiarisation, especially for those of us who had been on aeroplanes with rotary engines for many months. Unfamiliarity also seemed to increase the number of gremlins that beset us, and the gunnery was different too. The Lewis gun, mounted on the top plane, was of limited use. It was almost impossible to change a drum in a fight or while flying in close formation, as this required the gun to be released from its position and drawn down into the cockpit. Getting rid of the empty double drum in the slipstream was hazardous, and accurate flight, while replacing the drum and returning the gun to a firing position, was very difficult too.
>
> In order to give the squadron a better opportunity to get accustomed to the new machines, one flight at a time was given a week to ten days out of the frontline at Berck Plage, a former resort on the Channel coast, south of Calais. The increase in speed, especially in a dive, and greater ceiling for operational altitude made a great difference in the machine's potential, but it also put more strain on the pilot. I managed to get up to between 17,000–18,000ft, and later patrols were often maintained around 15,000ft. This greatly increased the pilot's level of discomfort from cold, adversely effect his ears and breathing.In early March, the squadron began to make its presence felt as an aggressive force up and down the lines. In fact, there were very few encounters behind our own lines, which accounted for the number of aircraft we claimed shot down out of control, but not officially confirmed. Rumours of a coming enemy offensive increased, and with them came increased tension. On one patrol with two flights we skirted a gala performance of 'Richthofen's Circus', which was then based across the lines from us at Douai. It was quite a show, the Germans in their multi-coloured Albatros scouts wheeling all over the sky, although we did not get into close combat.
>
> My flight commander, R S McClintock (who was also a five-victory ace), received the Military Cross during the first week of April. He was a good pilot with an excellent record in the squadron, but was inclined to be the remote Englishman, and I never felt quite at home with him, and probably thought he could have given more help and care for new pilots and their essential orientation to operational training. McClintock was promoted and transferred as CO to No. 3 Sqn, and on 20 April – my birthday – the flight was taken over by Capt Philip Scott Burge (also an ace, with 11 victories to his name), who chose me as his second in command. I was very much encouraged by his personality and leadership. This was just as well, for in May we were entering the most crucial month of aerial warfare. The machines were now under better maintenance and there were fewer frustrating returns from patrol, due to malfunction.

SE 5a D336 was flown by Lt Walter C. Daniel of No. 64 Sqn from Izel-le-Hameau during what was – certainly for him – the eventful month of May 1918. (Walter C. Daniel album via Jon Guttman)

On 3 May Burge, Daniel and 2Lt Bernard A Walkerdine (a six-victory ace) sent a Rumpler C down in flames near Mercatel. They saw the observer, Lt d R Fritz Perner of *Fl Abt (A)* 208, jump out, while his pilot, Gefr Hans Gaul, perished when the aircraft hit the ground. After suffering partial wing failure and aileron damage as he pulled out of a dive on the 16th, Daniel was injured in the subsequent crash landing. He spent a week in hospital and was then posted to Home Establishment and training duties on 30 May.

Robust though the SE 5a was, Daniel was fortunate to have survived his discovery that even this rugged fighter had its limitations. On 4 January 1918, Capt Frederick Hatherly Bruce Selous, commander of No. 60 Sqn's B Flight, was descending on an

Pilots of No. 60 Sqn in late 1917. They are, from left to right, Capt Robert Leslie Chidlaw-Roberts (ten victories), 2Lt William Edwin Jenkins (ten victories) and Capt Frederick Hatherly Bruce Selous. While returning from a patrol on 23 November 1917, the wings of 2Lts Jenkins' and Maurice West-Thompson's SE 5as dovetailed, causing both to fatally crash near Poperinghe. Selous died on 4 January 1918 when his wings failed while power-diving on a German two-seater at an estimated 300mph. (O. A. Sater Collection via Jon Guttman)

The British usually flew in V-shaped flights of three to seven aircraft in 1917, and would continue to do so until the Battle of Britain in 1940. German *Jastas* were generally divided into two *Ketten* of four or five each if they could muster full strength. How much cooperation occurred upon contact with the enemy was often determined by the leadership qualities of the flight or unit commander.

 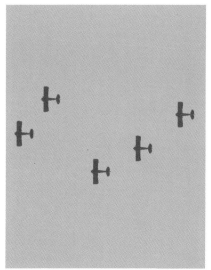

enemy two-seater in a steep power dive at an estimated 300mph when his SE 5a (C5334) suddenly shed its wings. He crashed to his death one-and-a-quarter miles east of Menin.

A later pilot who learned how much stress an SE 5a could handle was six-victory ace Lt Harris G. Clements, who was born in Kent but grew up in Canada before the war. Clements said he 'flew Maurice Farman Shorthorns – a fearsome machine – and then Pups and SE 5as', before being posted to No 74 Sqn, forming up at London Colney in February 1918. By then the SE 5a had come fully into its stride, and as an added bonus Clements got to enter combat under the experienced tutelage of Capt Edward 'Mick' Mannock:

He watched me coming in from a training flight with Lt J. I. T. 'Taffy' Jones. Jones, as was pretty usual, bounced in and broke a few bits of his machine. I landed smoothly – Mannock was impressed, asked me to join the flight and that was that.

In spite of the SE 5a's aptitude for diving hit-and-run attacks, Mannock believed in being ready for a close-range dogfight, and on one patrol, when no Germans turned up, he challenged Clements to an aerobatic competition in which each tried to out-stunt the other – and see just how much stress their planes could take. After Mannock's last high-speed turn, Clements found out:

After a quarter of a turn I felt a tremendous jolt and heard a slight cracking and snapping over the sound of my motor. I levelled out immediately, throttled back and signalled Mick that something was wrong. He played shepherd to me all the way home, watching for Huns and coming in close to watch for any signs of my machine coming apart.

My rigger rushed over and was about to explain what happened when I waved him away. It wasn't good for one's confidence to know much about such things – upon landing, my rigging had given way and the upper wing collapsed. Too much knowledge

RICHARD A. MAYBERY

At least ten SE 5/5a aces were credited with ten or more Albatros D Vs shot down, along with the earlier D IIIs, later fighter types and two-seaters as well. Based on British records, the greatest number of D Vs downed by an SE 5/5a pilot were the 19 credited to one of No. 56 Sqn's many paladins, Richard Aveline Maybery.

Born in Brecknock, South Wales, on 4 January 1895, Maybery was the only son of H. O. A. and Lucy Maybery. Although his father was a local barrister, Richard, after being educated at Connaught House in Weymouth and at Stanley, Wellington College (where he excelled in football and other sports), turned his back on the legal profession and chose soldiering as a career instead. He graduated fifth in his officers' training class at Sandhurst, winning first prize for field engineering, tactics and strategy. Maybery was then posted to the 21st Lancers in Rawalpindi, and served on India's Northwest Frontier. Badly wounded fighting Mohmands during the battle of Shabkadar on 5 September 1915, Maybery was unable to sit on his horse, so he transferred to the RFC.

After training in Egypt and England, he was posted to C Flight of No 56 Sqn in late June 1917. The unit's withdrawal to England for home defence from 23 June to 5 July gave Maybery time to become acquainted with and learn pointers from the unit's veterans.

Maybery soon proved his outstanding abilities as a marksman by driving down an Albatros D V near Hénin-Liétard for his first confirmed victory on 7 July – just days after the unit's return to France. Two more were credited to him on the 12th, 16th and the 23rd, along with a D III on the 27th. Now an ace, Maybery finished the month off with an epic sortie on the 31st during which he attacked the German aerodrome at Heule, hitting its sheds with the first three 20lb Cooper bombs dropped from a No. 56 Sqn SE 5. He saved his fourth weapon for the Courtrai railway station, after which he strafed *Jasta* 4's aerodrome at Cuerne, attacked a train, shot up an infantry column and used the last of his ammunition to down a two-seater near Wevelghem. More D Vs fell to Maybery over the next four months, during which time he also received the Military Cross and Bar, was promoted to captain and, on 19 November, put in command of A Flight

when Capt R. T. C. Hoidge was transferred to Home Establishment.

On 19 December A and B Flights scrapped with a mixed bag of 'V-strutters', and Maybery was last seen pursuing an already burning D V over Bourlon Wood. German *K-Flakbatterie* 108 subsequently reported that he had fallen victim to one of its lorry-mounted anti-aircraft guns sited some 600 yards south of Haynecourt. The British ace was buried by gunners from the flak battery that had shot him down. Maybery's demise may have also been credited to Vfw Artur Weber of *Jasta* 5, who claimed an SE 5a near Havrincout Wood.

As for Maybery's 21st, and last, victory, *Jasta* 20 recorded that Ltn Walter Braun came down near Faumont (not far from Bourlon Wood) at 1405 hrs on 19 December, and died of his wounds at Dourges the following day.

Upon learning of his death, No. 56 Sqn CO Maj R. G. Blomfield stated 'Capt Maybery was, I think, the bravest, most dashing air fighter I have ever come across, and, of course, his career has been brilliant. He was so brilliant, so popular and always so cheerful. He set a wonderful example to the newer pilots. He was almost too brave, and I do not think I have ever met a man so capable. He was good at absolutely everything.'

can be a dangerous thing in certain cases. We flew with our trust in our mechanics to fortify our confidence, confidence being so important in air fighting.

Clements certainly had confidence in his Viper-engined SE 5a:

It was a terrific machine – strong and reliable. The cockpit was warm and almost draught free. You could light a match in there. Indeed, Mick used to light his pipe sometimes when he was returning from a patrol.

Capt Edward V. Mannock, in the cockpit of his 'A'-marked SE 5a D276 whilst serving as A Flight commander of the newly formed No. 74 Sqn, prepares to depart for France on 31 March 1918. Mannock's inspiring, but mature, leadership quickly turned his unit into one of the most successful in the RAF. (Jon Guttman)

Although high-scoring aces Mannock and Capt Keith L. 'Grid' Caldwell, who had transferred to No. 74 Sqn from No. 60 Sqn, touted the SE 5a as a first-rate fighter to the new pilots, Clements noted that they, like Daniel in No. 64 Sqn, privately criticised its armament of two different machine guns. 'They could not understand why twin Vickers hadn't been fitted', he said. 'Both thought that the Sopwith Dolphin (which indeed had twin Vickers guns) was the superior machine.'

'The Lewis was a damned nuisance' agreed ten-victory ace Robert Leslie Chidlaw-Roberts, who had served alongside Caldwell in No 60. Sqn;

You pulled it down to get under two-seaters, but the only one who really used it like that was McCudden, who always attacked from underneath. Personally, I would have preferred two Vickers – less knobs to play about with when you had to change a drum. With the Vickers, of course, you had a belt, and I think it was slightly more reliable. We had a double drum on the Lewis, but the gun was only built for a single, which may have made it jam easier. If you were very good with your hands you could correct a jam, but I wasn't very clever. I used to get fed up with the Lewis.

Of course, the unsung essentials to pilots on both sides were the riggers, fitters and armourers. 'When I had a flight I had the same flight sergeant and corporal', Chidlaw-Roberts recalled. 'In fact, when I left No. 60 Sqn we wept together my sergeant and I – we had become very fond of each other. They worked like devils and never grumbled. They were absolutely marvellous, yet we pilots had all the honour and glory'.

LUFTSTREITSKRÄFTE

While RFC pilots were initially sceptical of the SE 5, their Germans counterparts took possession of their Albatros D Vs with unmitigated disappointment for the scant improvement in performance it offered over the D III, and the even greater fragility of its wing cellule. Even so, their chagrin was not paralysing. The tactics required to make the most of the D III's strengths and avoid its weaknesses also largely applied to the D Vs too, so there was little adjusting to do – just making the most of what they had, while wondering when a really improved fighter would reach them at the front.

Ranking SE 5/5a ace James McCudden, whose memoir *Five Years in the Royal Flying Corps* combined patriotism with hard factual observations, had the privilege of trying out his principal aerial opposition in November 1917:

> On 5 November I went to Hendon with Capt Clive Collett to fly a V-Strutter Albatros which he had for demonstration purposes, and I had a nice ride in it, but I could not think how the German pilots could manoeuvre them so well, for they were certainly not easy to handle.

The average German fighter pilot had already served in a reconnaissance or bombing unit before requesting a transfer, or being seconded due to displays of aggressiveness, to one of the two German fighter schools. For example, Hans-Georg von der Osten had served with the 3rd Ulhlan Guard Regiment in Flanders and in the Pinsk Marshes, in Russia, before an interest in aviation led to his applying, and entering, flight training with *Flieger Erstaz Abteilung (FEA)* 6 at Darmstadt in February 1916. After flying two-seaters with *Fl Abt* 69 on the Eastern Front that autumn, in

Vfw Paul Billik with his early Albatros D V of *Jasta* 12. Later serving in *Jasta* 7, Billik had been credited with eight victories by the time he was commissioned as a leutnant and given command of *Jasta* 52 – an *Amerikaprogramm* unit that had a mixed bag of Albatros and Pfalz scouts – on 27 December 1917. Billik was apparently flying an Albatros D Va when he opened the *Staffel's* account with a double victory over SE 5as on 9 March 1918, bringing down the commander of No. 40 Sqn, Maj Richard J. Tilney (who died of his wounds on the 12th) and Lt P. LaT Foster, who was taken prisoner. Billik's tally stood at 31 when he was shot down and taken prisoner on 10 August 1918. (Jon Guttman)

November von der Osten took single-seat fighter training in Warsaw. 'After that,' he said, 'I did a short "guest" performance with the Austrian Szumai Corps as a fighter pilot without ever catching sight of a Russian aeroplane.'

Ordered home due to illness, von der Osten became an airfield controller at *FEA* 4 at Breslau-Gandau until June 1917, when Manfred von Richthofen landed there and the two became acquainted. That led to the latter submitting a request for him to join *Jasta* 11. On 1 August von der Osten recalled:

I received my orders to join *Jagdgeschwader* Nr 1, *Jasta* 11, with a detour en route via the *Jasta* school at Valenciennes. There, I flew zealously for three days. I was given another student with whom I was to practice formation flying. I don't think we practiced formation flying with more than two aircraft. Then we practiced target shooting, which consisted only of shooting at ground targets. I don't remember any lectures, but I think I remember Oblt Ernst von Althaus (a nine-victory ace), in a green Hussar uniform, there as an instructor.

From there von der Osten joined *Jasta* 11 at Marckebeeke on 10 August. The *Staffelführer*, Oblt Wilhelm Reinhard, immediately ordered him to give a demonstration flight upon his arrival:

We were not required to do aerobatics at this time. I took the opportunity to fly over Kortijk and saw the places where, three years earlier in 1914, I had been quartered with my regiment. When I landed, Reinhard was still standing there, and he said, 'Yes, you'll do'.

JG I *Kommandeur* Rittm von Richthofen with personnel of his old *Jasta* 11. They are, from left to right (with victories in parentheses), Ltn d R Siegfried Gussmann (5), Fw Ltn Fritz Schubert, technical officer (3), Ltn Hans-Georg von der Osten (5), Ltn Werner Steinhäuser (10), von Richthofen (80), Ltn Karl Esser, Ltn Eduard Lübbert, Oblt Hans-Helmut Boddien (5), Ltn Hans-Karl von Linsingen, Ltn Eberhardt Mohnicke (9) and Vfw Edgar Scholz (6). (National Archives)

OTTO KÖNNECKE

Late in 1917, No. 56 Sqn ace Capt James McCudden frequently encountered a skillfully flown Albatros D V that he called 'Greentail'. Unbeknownst to him, his worthy foe came from a *Jagdstaffel* that identified all of its aircraft with red noses and green tail surfaces edged in red – *Jasta* 5. Among the pilots in that unit who is known to have battled 'Fighting Fifty-Six' was a lesser-known ace named Otto Könnecke.

Born in Strasbourg on 20 September 1892, Könnecke graduated from the Building Trade School at Frankfort am Main as a carpenter's assistant, but in 1911 he chose military service with Railroad Regiment Nr 3 at Hanau. Acquiring an interest in aviation, in 1913 he began pilot training at *Flieger Erstaz Abtilung* 4 at Metz. Könnecke subsequently served as a flying instructor from the outbreak of war in July 1914 through to 3 December 1916, when he was shipped off to *Jasta* 25 in Macedonia. After scoring an unconfirmed victory on 9 January 1917, Könnecke was credited with downing Serbian Farmans on 5 and 6 February, gaining him a transfer to the Western Front. From *Armee Flugpark* 2, he was assigned to *Jasta* 5 in April 1917. Re-opening his account with an FE 2d on 28 May, Könnecke soon became one of the unit's 'Golden Triumvirate', alongside aces Josef Mai and Fritz Rumey.

Könnecke's first SE 5a was claimed during a scrap with No. 56 Sqn over Tilloy at 1430 hrs on 28 January 1918. This may have been a case of overoptimistic or multiple perception, however, for the British unit's only loss – SE 5a B610 – was the result of its losing a fight with a two-seater crewed by Ltns Schuppau and Schandva of *Fl Abt (A)* 233, Lt Lester J. Williams being taken prisoner.

Könnecke's next success occurred on 1 April when Lt Frank Beaumont of No. 56 Sqn fired a green light to indicate mechanical problems, dropped out of his patrol and headed west, only to be picked off by Könnecke at 1245 hrs and driven down near Albert and captured. An SE 5a claimed at 1715 hrs on 11 April was probably the machine flown by Capt Kelvin Crawford of No. 60 Sqn, who was firing at a two-seater when Könnecke intervened and killed him near Bucquoy. At 1850 hrs the very next day Könnecke downed a fourth SE 5a north of Albert, which may have been the fighter flown by 2Lt E T Hendrie of No. 24 Sqn, who was wounded but made it to Allied lines.

Könnecke would be credited with six more SE 5as destroyed after *Jasta* 5 re-equipped with the vastly superior Fokker D VII in May. On the 12th of that same month he was awarded the Golden Military Merit Cross, and on 15 June he was commissioned as a leutnant. On 20 July Könnecke received the Knight's Cross with Swords of the Royal Hohenzollern House Order, and on 26 September, with his score at 32, he was awarded the coveted *Orden Pour le Mérite*. An SE 5a on 18 October and DH 4s on 1 and 4 November took his final victory tally to 35.

Post-war, Könnecke served as a pilot for *Deutsche Luft Hansa* from the airline's inception in 1926, and after joining the Luftwaffe in 1935, he rose to the rank of major, commanding various flying schools. After World War II, Könnecke remained in Germany until his death on 25 January 1956.

After sticking close to Reinhard on the first few sorties, von der Osten claimed that 'by the third day I was having tougher air fights on my own'. At 2015 hrs on 17 August he attacked what he thought were Sopwith two-seaters, but which turned out to be Bristol F 2Bs of No. 22 Sqn:

I had the opportunity to attack one of them from below at a favourable angle, which forced him to go immediately into a spiralling gliding descent. I pursued him, firing several bursts through the clouds until he landed with a crash in the area of Staden. I heard later that the observer was killed and the pilot badly wounded.

During the air fight I had seen a German navy fighter join us beneath the clouds, and I watched him fly close over the crashed Englishman and drop a message-bag with his address. He subsequently claimed to have scored the victory, but he was contradicted by the statements of the wounded pilot, who stated emphatically that he had been shot down by 'the Red Baron'.

The British pilot who mistook von der Osten's red-nosed Albatros D V for von Richthofen's, 2Lt R. S. Phelan, was taken prisoner – his observer, Lt J. L. MacFarlane, had indeed died in the fight. That evening, von Richthofen ordered a bottle of champagne because von der Osten's first victory had also been *Jasta* 11's 200th. Von der Osten stated that drinking was a rarity at *Jasta* 11, because 'we always had to keep ourselves ready for action', although at neighbouring *Jasta* 4, under Oblt Kurt von Döring, 'they sometimes had some very wet evenings'.

Ltn von der Osten's fifth, and last, victory was over an SE 5a near Havrincourt on 15 December 1917, which he said 'took place at rather long range, as I could not overtake the enemy aeroplane, which was much faster. I fired and emptied both my guns at him, and then saw my opponent touch down in a crash landing.' His victim, 2Lt Geoffrey Walker of No. 56 Sqn, was injured in SE 5a B63. Having come down in Havrincourt Wood, which was within Allied lines, Walker was immediately taken to No. 8 General Hospital.

'These SE 5s were our nastiest opponents due to their speed and their climbing ability,' von der Osten recalled during an interveiw in 1974. 'Because of their excellent British engines, they were much better than our aeroplanes. You could tell this immediately since they hummed so evenly when in flight, while our engines rattled like one of today's Volkswagen engines.'

A typical *Jagdstaffel* consisted of 12 flying officers, mostly leutnants or oberleutnants, and about 80 non-flying support personnel ranging from flieger (private) to offizierstellvertreter (roughly the equivalent of a warrant officer). The commissioned and non-commissioned personnel lived separately, with the officers' quarters ranging from tents to châteaux, if available. The support personnel, however, usually lived in large pentagonal tents that had been erected within walking distance of the airfield.

The other principal difference between ranks was the turnover rate. While combat attrition among the flying officers could be high, *Jasta* 4, for example, recorded the loss of only eight of its eighty ground crewmen throughout the war. Four were slain in a British bombing raid on 20 September 1917, one killed and one wounded in an accident while testing machine guns and two unteroffiziere court-martialled and sentenced to two years' imprisonment for assaulting an army hauptmann during the course of a nocturnal attempt to steal his geese!

Contrary to British lore that JG I had its own train to move from one hot spot to the next like a travelling circus, the standard procedure for a *Jasta* move – including JG I's – involved a day spent loading its four lorries, along with eight borrowed trucks from the local army unit. The *Jasta* would then take anywhere from one to five days to drive its ground personnel, tents and equipment to the new aerodrome, while the pilots flew the aeroplanes there. About half a day was spent re-establishing the unit at its new location.

Depending on the town and its environs, JG I's four *Staffeln* could occupy as many as four separate fields, usually within a two-mile radius. Some items, such as six anti-aircraft guns per *Staffel*, along with the soldiers who manned them, chaplains and legal support if courts-martial came up, were supplied by the *Armee* to which the *Jasta* was assigned.

The most notable aspect of German fighter activity throughout 1917 was its emphasis on defence. *Jagdflieger* often referred to British airmen as being more 'sporting' than the French, unaware of the fact that their aggressive OPs were dictated more by policy than knight-errantry. Similarly, a British pilot ignorant of the *Jastas'* tactical dicta might have questioned German courage.

'Well, at that time we didn't realise that they had orders not to cross the lines', explained ten-victory ace Robert L. Chidlaw-Roberts of No. 60 Sqn. 'We thought that it was rather a poor show. I've read since, however, that they were just obeying orders not to come across, as they didn't want to lose too many machines. They were a fine lot really, much the same as ourselves. We had a very clean war, and there was very little in it.'

Even at the time, James McCudden of No. 56 Sqn was capable of appraising his foes fairly and individually, knowing that taking each one's measure meant survival in any given fight. In his memoir he transcended the rancorous Allied propaganda of 1918 to give a general impression of the 'wily Hun':

The German aviator is disciplined, resolute and brave, and is a foeman worthy of our best. I have had many opportunities to study his psychology since the war commenced, and although I have seen some cases where a German aviator has, on occasion, been a coward, I have, on the other hand, seen many incidents which have given me food for thought, and have caused me to respect the German aviator. The more I fight them the more I respect them for their fighting qualities.

I have on many occasions had German machines at my mercy over our lines, and they have had the choice of landing and being taken prisoner or being shot down. With one exception they chose the latter path.

Further, it is foolish to disparage the powers of the German aviator, for doing so must necessarily belittle the efforts of our own brave boys, whose duty it is to fight them at every possible opportunity.

COMBAT

When the Albatros D V reached the front at the end of May 1917, No. 56 Sqn's pilots were still in the process of developing the SE 5's potential as a fighter – and so was the Royal Aircraft Factory with the more powerful SE 5a. The Germans had generally adapted to the Albatros D III, with its reinforced wing cellule, and had flown it to deadly effect throughout 'Bloody April', as well as during the two following months.

Indeed, Manfred von Richthofen was still flying a D III when he scored his 53rd victory on 18 June, but was at the controls of D V 1177/17 when he destroyed a

Rittm Manfred von Richthofen visits naval personnel in Flanders in his Albatros D V. (Greg VanWyngarden)

SPAD VII of No. 23 Sqn five days later. He downed a DH 4 on the 24th and an RE 8 on the 25th, which was also the day he officially took charge of JG I and passed command of *Jasta* 11 to Ltn Karl Allmenröder.

On 1 July 1917, Oblt Adolf *Ritter* von Tutschek, commander of *Jasta* 12, wrote that the *Flugpark* had notified him of 'four new Albatros ready and waiting for my *Jagdstaffel*, and would I please pick them up'. The next day he noted, 'Picked up my new Albatros D V 2005/17 from the park yesterday and have made six flights since then.'

Unforeseen problems with the new 200hp Hispano-Suiza engine delayed the arrival of SE 5as at No. 56 Sqn, and the concurrent transfer of its older aeroplanes to No. 60 Sqn, until 8 July. Only five had reached the second SE 5 unit by 3 August, and the first No. 60 Sqn pilots to fly them, aces Capts William A. Bishop and Keith L. Caldwell, were as unsure of their advantages over the tried and true Nieuport 17s and 23s as Albert Ball of No. 56 Sqn had been back in March. Moreover, the Wolseley-built Hispano-Suiza engines were proving troublesome. Since commencing operations in the SE 5s on 23 July, No. 60 Sqn's pilots had reported three engine failures within the space of just a week.

The unit was still under orders not to venture over German territory when, on 29 July, Bishop, Lt Frederick O. Soden and 2Lt Graham C. Young spotted three Albatros D IIIs flying tantalisingly close to the frontline. Bishop attacked, two of the Germans fled and he claimed to have shot the remaining one down in flames over Phalempin at 1810 hrs, although the Germans have no matching casualty for that time and place. The next day saw the first encounter between No. 60 Sqn's SE 5s and Albatros D Vs, which illustrated the two new types' abilities, limitations and the importance of skill and tactics for the men who flew both. Capts Caldwell and Bishop and 2Lt W. H. Gunner were patrolling over Beaumont when they spotted a German two-seater, but they hesitated to attack it. Their suspicions were justified when four of *Jasta* 12's D Vs dived on them out of the sun. Bishop subsequently recalled in his memoir, *Winged Warfare*:

On 5 October 1917, SE 5a B507 of No. 60 Sqn was forced to land due to engine failure at *Jasta* 18's Harlebeeke aerodrome. Its pilot, 2Lt J. J. Fitzgerald, was taken prisoner. (Greg VanWyngarden)

A true combat veteran, New Zealander Maj Keith L. 'Grid' Caldwell DFC and Bar MC survived the war with 25 victories to his name. Some 17 of these came in the SE 5a, which he flew with Nos 60 and 74 Sqn. (Norman Franks)

Winner of the VC, DSO and Bar, MC, DFC, *Legion d'Honneur* and the *Croix de Guerre*, William Avery Bishop was, controversially, the highest-scoring Canadian ace of World War I with 72 victories. This tally saw him ranked first on the list of British and Empire aces. Bishop regularly clashed with Albatros D V/Vas during the latter half of 1917 while flying SE 5s with No. 60 Sqn (Bruce Robertson)

They approached, obviously with the intention of attacking us, but when only 300 yards away they recognised the machines we were flying and turned away quickly. They had been looking for easier prey, and were not very anxious for battle. We went after them though, and there followed a merry scrap. One of my trio, by some misfortune, got mixed up in a bad position and he was not seen again. He must have gone down.

Bishop was referring to Gunner, who was suffering from a faltering engine when Oblt von Tutschek attacked and shot him down in flames (for his 21st of 27 victories) near Hénin-Liétard. Caldwell was firing at another Albatros when his guns jammed and two others got onto his tail. Diving and desperate manoeuvring shook them off, by which time Caldwell was just 80ft above the ground. Bishop continued:

Then, looking back from the lines, Caldwell saw the fight going on some distance away over German-held territory, and realising that I was alone in the middle of it, he came back all the way, without either of his guns in working order. I still think it one of the bravest deeds I have ever heard of, as he had a hard time getting back to me, and then also in escaping for a second time.

I, for my part, was having the time of my life. The original four enemy scouts had been joined by three others, and picking out one that was higher than the rest, I concentrated on him and got to within 50 yards before I opened fire. He immediately turned over on his back, righted himself, turned over on his back again and then fell away completely out of control.

Seeing a thunderstorm approaching, Bishop finally disengaged, and with Caldwell he returned to Filescamp Farm aerodrome. They landed just ten minutes before the storm broke. After clearing his weapons, Caldwell flew another sortie that evening, without result.

Another guest of *Jasta* 18 was 2Lt Theodore Vernon-Lord of No. 84 Sqn. During the unit's first combat sortie on 15 October 1917 – bombing Harlebeeke – Lt Edward O. Krohn claimed an Albatros D V, but at 1315 hrs Vernon-Lord's SE 5a B574 'F' suffered a broken pushrod and he was forced to land at the very aerodrome he had just attacked. (Greg VanWyngarden)

Although Bishop was credited with the 'Out Of Control' Albatros as his 38th victory, *Jasta* 12 recorded no men or aeroplanes lost. That same day the German high command congratulated von Tutschek for reasons he described in a letter home:

> Today mother shall get a letter on extra special paper. I have a colossal respect for myself, and it seems I have become a 'big shot'. Yesterday at 0750 hrs I downed a triplane near Méricourt. At 1000 hrs a Nieuport fighter near Lievin and today at 0800 hrs a new SE 5 at Hénin-Liétard. They went down burning on this side. With that one I personally scored the 100th aerial victory of the *Staffel* in my black Albatros. They were verified through *Kogenluft* as the 19th, 20th and 21st victorious air combats.

Content though he seemed with himself and with his new Albatros, von Tutschek struck up a different tune in a letter on 1 August:

> In the past four weeks three new types of enemy aircraft have appeared. They are without a doubt far superior in their ability to climb than the best D V. They are the new English SE 5 single-seater, the 200hp SPAD and the very outstanding Bristol Fighter two-seater. While the Albatros D III and D V come near in their ability to climb with the Sopwith and Nieuport, and even surpass them in speed, it is almost impossible for them to force an SE 5 or a 200hp SPAD to fight because the enemy is able to avoid it by the ability of his craft to outclimb the Albatros.

After describing the Bristol as 'our most dangerous opponent', von Tutschek got down to cases, speaking for virtually every German fighter pilot on the Western Front:

> In my opinion a machine superior to these three would be more important than an increase in the number of the present ones. I can achieve more with three pilots and aeroplanes that are completely trustworthy, as good or better than the opposition in climbing, manoeuvrability and sturdiness, than I can with 20 pilots in D Vs of whose ability and performance I am not convinced, and must watch with apprehension while diving during air battle.

RUN-INS WITH THE 'CIRCUS'

The British offensives of 1917 were punctuated by numerous sharp, violent clashes between SE 5s and Albatros, of which only a handful of cases need be cited here to exemplify their nature. These encounters often involved No. 56 Sqn, whose pilots by September had evolved with their SE 5s and SE 5as into a well-honed team of veteran flights, experienced men and well-developed machines, against equally seasoned *Jagdstaffeln*, including those in JG I.

'Fighting Fifty-Six' had a couple of run-ins with the 'Richthofen Circus' on 14 September, starting with an 0805 hrs patrol led by ace Capt Geoffrey Hilton Bowman that encountered eight Albatros over Zandvoorde. The Germans scattered under C Flight's attack and Bowman chased an Albatros into a cloud. Upon emerging from

OVERLEAF
This early encounter between SE 5s and Albatros D Vs illustrated the two new types' strengths, limitations and the importance of skill and tactics for the men who flew both aeroplanes. On 29 July 1917, three SE 5s of No. 60 Sqn, flown by Capt Keith Caldwell, Capt William A. Bishop and 2Lt W. H. Gunner, were patrolling over Beaumont when they spotted a German two-seater. Veterans Bishop and Caldwell suspected a trap, so they held off their attack for a few minutes. Their suspicions were soon justified when four new Albatros D Vs of *Jagdstaffel* 12 dived out of the sun on them. In the ensuing fight Gunner suffered from engine trouble, and as he tried to flee the engagement, *Jasta* 12's commander, Oblt Adolf *Ritter* von Tutschek, swiftly took advantage of the opportunity. In spite of Caldwell's and Bishop's attempt to intervene, the German ace sent Gunner down in flames near Henin-Liétard for his 21st success and his unit's 100th victory. As the fight continued, 'Billy' Bishop drove an Albatros down out of control – credited to him as his 38th of an eventual 72 victories – but he was hard-pressed by the others. In spite of jammed guns, however, 'Grid' Caldwell climbed to assist Bishop, and their mutual support eventually drove off the enemy scouts, allowing No.60 Sqn aces to return to Filescamp Farm aerodrome.

MARK POSTLETHWAITE '04

it, he spotted his quarry 100 yards away, fleeing east. Keeping to the edge of the cloud, Bowman stalked it until he caught it – apparently by surprise – and a volley 'at very close range' sent the scout down to crash in a field a mile northwest of Menin. Bowman's victim, Ltn Gisbert-Wilhelm Groos of *Jasta* 11, was slightly wounded.

Elsewhere, fellow ace Lt Robert Sloley sent a red-nosed Albatros spinning down, only to see it flatten out and fly eastward. He then claimed an Albatros, painted grey with a blue tail, out of control. A well-placed shot in his engine compelled ace Capt Reggie Hoidge to force-land north of Zillebeke Lake, but *Jasta* 11 did not claim him.

Eleven more of No. 56 Sqn's SE 5as took off at 1700 hrs, and a short while later Capt McCudden's B Flight dived on seven Albatros over Roulers. 'I picked out my target and fired a burst from my Lewis', McCudden wrote. 'I watched this Hun in a spiral down to about 4,000ft over Ledeghem, but after that I lost sight of him as he was so low'. Credited as 'driven down', McCudden's opponent was apparently a slightly wounded Oblt Ernst Weigand, *Jasta* 10's deputy commander, who, between scoring three victories, also performed the administrative tasks that his *Staffelführer*, Ltn Werner Voss, disdained.

McCudden next attacked a pair of two-seaters and nearly collided with one, but failed to bring it down. He then found a *Staffel* of Albatros standing between him and Allied lines:

Immediately I did the best thing possible. I opened out my engine full and charged right through the middle of them, firing both guns and pulling my controls about all over the place in order to spray my bullets about as much as possible. The old Huns seemed to scratch their heads and say 'What the devil next?' I very soon outdistanced them owing to my superior speed, for the SE, with engine full on and dropping a little height, is very fast indeed.

High-scoring ace Arthur Percival Foley Rhys Davids saw much action in the SE 5/5a with No. 56 Sqn up until his death in action on 27 October 1917, when he became the fifth victim of *Jasta* 'Boelcke' Albatros D V ace Ltn Karl Gallwitz. Fellow ace McCudden wrote of Rhys Davids, 'If one was ever over the Salient in the autumn of 1917 and saw an SE 5 fighting like Hell amidst a heap of Huns, one would find nine times out of ten that the SE was flown by Rhys Davids.' (Alex Revell)

With his retreat option restored, McCudden flew south to Polygon Wood, where he met fellow ace 2Lt Arthur Rhys Davids. They spotted a dozen Albatros over Gheluve and circled about under them, trying to draw them westward. When a reinforcing flight of No. 56 Sqn SE 5as arrived, McCudden laid into the Germans, but soon found them to be competent opponents.

After last seeing Rhys Davids 'fighting a very skilful Hun, whose Albatros was painted with a red nose, a green fuselage and a silver tail', McCudden 'had just finished chasing a Hun around when I saw an SE hurtle by in a streaming cloud of white vapour – apparently hot water or petrol'. Spotting a lone Albatros flying south between two cloud banks, he thought, 'By Jove, here's a sitter!' But as he closed to firing range, he heard gunfire behind and looked back to see 'three red noses coming for me'. Diving from 9,000ft to 3,000ft, in the course of an eight-mile chase McCudden widened the distance between himself and his pursuers 'from 100 yards to a mile', and made his way home. There, he learned that 'it was Rhys Davids whom I had seen go into a cloud, emitting volumes of petrol vapour, and he was very lucky not to have been set on fire by the flame from his exhaust'.

Switching to his gravity tank, Rhys Davids made it to Bailleul aerodrome, being claimed by, but not confirmed to, Ltn Julius Schmidt of *Jasta* 3. Less fortunate in the fight was 2Lt Norman H. Crowe, who was shot down and killed in SE 5a B516 by Vfw Karl Menckhoff for his 11th victory.

LEARNING BY EXPERIENCE

An example of how experience and familiarity with one's aeroplane's abilities and limitations could trump the inherent advantages of an opposing machine was illustrated in an encounter between Albatros D Vs and SE 5as of No. 84 Sqn on 31 October 1917. The third SE 5a-equipped unit, No. 84 Sqn had been in action for just two weeks by the 31st when Capt Kenneth Malice St Clair Graeme Leask, in B579, led five aeroplanes of his A Flight in an attack on four German scouts, only to be jumped by 12 more.

In the ensuing melee Leask and 2Lt John Steele Ralston, in B4853, were credited with Albatros D Vs out of control over Menin at 1540 hrs – Leask's third of an eventual eight victories and Ralston's second of twelve. However, two of the flight, 2Lts Edward W. Powell and George R. Gray, failed to return. Powell may have been killed by Ltn Heinrich Bongartz of *Jasta* 36, who claimed an SE 5a south of Roulers at 1610 hrs German time for his 20th victory (and his third for the day). Gray's fate was described by his opponent, Ltn d R Erwin Böhme, CO of *Jasta* 'Boelcke':

High above us an English fighter squadron was swarming about. We tried to climb as quickly as possible. Because I had used most of my fuel on my flight home, my aircraft was quite light and rose like Charlemagne. In a few moments I was high above my comrade. I climbed directly toward the English, who flew ever higher, keeping them in front of me and constantly in my sight.

Royal Aircraft Factory-built SE 5a B4876 was powered by a 200hp Hispano-Suiza engine when it went to France with No. 84 Sqn on 21 September 1917. It failed to return from an OP on 20 October, having last been seen flying southwest between Roulers and the lines northwest of Ypres. The pilot, 2Lt W. E. Watts, was later reported as a PoW. (Greg VanWyngarden)

Finally, one of them had the insipid idea to come down and attack me from above. I foiled his first attack by closing rapidly with him, head-on. Because of that he immediately yanked his aircraft up and was quickly about 200 metres above me again. He flew the newest type of aircraft, with a very powerful motor. From then on he made four or five unskilled attempts to attack, but each time I quickly positioned myself vertically under him so that he could not obtain a line of fire on me. At the same time he gradually began to lose height, and at an opportune moment I turned the tables on him. Now the foolish fellow lies below! The entire encounter did not last five minutes. Indeed, it certainly could not have lasted much longer, as I reached my airfield without any fuel.

The Germans recovered SE 5a B544 roughly intact, but Gray died of his wounds soon after, having become the 21st of 24 victories for Böhme. The latter was himself killed attacking an Armstrong-Whitworth FK 8 on 29 November.

No. 84 Sqn's CO, Maj William Sholto Douglas, summed up the situation at the time:

All through October we fought up and down the Menin-Roulers Road to the east of Ypres. It was a hard school for a new and untried squadron,

SE 5a FUSELAGE AND WING GUNS

Both the SE 5 and SE 5a had two different machine guns. A 0.303-in Vickers gun was enclosed in the left fuselage, with a Hyland Type E loading handle and a Fitzgerald jam clearer. It was synchronised to fire 400 rounds of belt-fed ammunition through the propeller using Constantinesco CC hydraulic interrupter gear. The 0.303-in Lewis gun on a Foster mounting above the upper wing could be pulled down for reloading. It fired ammunition drawn from double drum magazines developed by pioneer RFC ace Maj Lanoe G. Hawker, which increased the original drum's capacity from 47 to 97 rounds.

OPPOSITE
Describing his combat of
31 October 1917, Ltn Erwin
Böhme of *Jasta* 'Boelcke'
gave some insight into how
experienced German airmen
made the most of their
Albatros D Vs against the
inherently better SE 5a. (IWM
Q107385 via Jon Guttman)

LEFT
SE 5as of No. 84 Sqn lie in
durance vile on *Jasta* 17's
airfield at Wasquehal. B544 'E'
was flown by 2Lt George R.
Gray, who was shot down
southeast of Zillebeke Lake
by Ltn Böhme and died of his
wounds on 31 October 1917.
B566 'J' was last seen two
miles east of Ypres on 28
October, 2Lt A. W. Rush
becoming a PoW. (Greg
VanWyngarden)

and at first, owing to the inexperience of the pilots, we suffered casualties. But bitter experience is a quick teacher.

THE RED BARON'S FIRST SE 5a KILL

Manfred von Richthofen did not add an SE 5a to his already considerable score until 30 November 1917 – the day the Germans counterattacked to retake some of the ground lost to the last British offensive along the Cambrai Front. The 'Red Baron' had

ALBATROS D V
FUSELAGE GUNS

As with its predecessors since the D I,
the Albatros D V was armed with twin
7.92mm LMG 08/15 machine guns
with 500 rounds of ammunition each.
Both the D V's Hedke interrupter gear
and the improved Semmler gear that
synchronised the D Va's guns were
developed by Albatros factory
Werkmeisters.

scored seven previous victories over other types in his unloved D V since 23 June 1917, although he had spent almost three weeks in hospital after suffering a head wound during an encounter with FE 2ds of No. 20 Sqn on 6 July. He had also tried out a preproduction Fokker F I, bringing down an RE 8 on 1 September and a Sopwith Pup two days later, but on the 15th a Sopwith Camel shot the new triplane down, killing his friend, and 33-victory ace, Oblt Kurt Wolff.

Von Richthofen was flying D V 4693/17, with a red engine cowl, fuselage and tail, when he resumed his scoring on 23 November with a DH 5 – Lt James A. V. Boddy of No. 64 Sqn survived the crash in British lines but lost a leg. Then, on the 30th, the Baron led his brother Lothar and Ltn Siegfried Gussmann against what he described as ten single-seaters over the frontline trenches at 1430 hrs. 'After I had fired at several Englishmen', he wrote, 'I fired from close range behind a single-seater, which after 100 rounds crashed in flames in the vicinity of Steinbruch Forest'.

Von Richthofen's opponents came from No. 41 Sqn, which had replaced the last of its DH 5s with SE 5as on 7 November, just in time for the Cambrai offensive. At 1300 hrs Loudon James MacLean, promoted to captain the day before, led a close OP from Léalvillers aerodrome, and 30 minutes later he spotted two red-painted Albatros scouts flying at about 2,000ft over Inchy-en-Artois. Joined by Lt Donald Argyle Douglas Ian Macgregor, MacLean attacked an Albatros, and after firing 30 rounds saw it spin into the ground. He then joined his wingman against the other German, coming at it from the front while Macgregor attacked from the rear. The D V pilot, however, refused to give way, compelling MacLean to go into an abrupt climb to avoid a collision. As he turned to resume the fight, he saw Macgregor's SE 5a, B644, going down in flames and the Albatros retiring to the northeast.

Nearby, Lt Russell Winnicott fired at an Albatros and then turned into a cloud, and upon diving out of it he too saw Macgregor's flaming descent. Spotting another red Albatros, Winnicott dived on it and kept firing until he saw it turn over and crash near Fontaine. Fifteen minutes later Capt Meredith Thomas claimed an Albatros that he had picked out of a formation of six, and at which he fired almost 350 rounds until it crashed east of Rumilly.

In spite of the No. 41 Sqn pilots making two claims, neither von Richthofen's brother nor Gussmann were casualties in the fight. The latter in fact was credited with a 'DH 5' 15 minutes later, which may actually have been 2Lt Ernest F H Davis' SE 5a – the fighter was hit in several places but made it back to Léalvillers. Macgregor's body was never recovered, the pilot having become von Richthofen's 63rd victory, and his last in an Albatros. The Baron's next 17, including two more SE 5as, would be scored in 1918 in Fokker Dr Is.

DEATH OF 'GREENTAIL'

One of the more famous Albatros D Vs acquired its notoriety through Maj James McCuddens' memoir, *Five Years in the Royal Flying Corps*, which described several clashes with a skilled German that, for want of any other identification, he called 'Greentail'. McCudden was unaware that at that time green tails trimmed in red, along with red noses, were the standard markings for *Jasta* 5, and that he was probably fighting more than one pilot from that crack unit.

On 19 December 1917, McCudden's B Flight and Capt R. A. Maybery's A Flight had a sprawling melee near Bourlon Wood with Albatros D Vs and a few Pfalz D IIIs of *Jastas* 5 and 20, during which McCudden's flight encountered 'Greentail' and a brown Pfalz. The ace wrote in his book:

> We scrapped these two for over half-an-hour, and with no result, for they cooperated wonderfully and put up a magnificent show – we could not attack either of them without having the other after us. There were now only three of us, and we did our very best to get one of them, but to no avail. After a time they both went down, apparently for some more petrol or ammunition, and we flew home.

Maybery did not return from the patrol and was reported missing that night. '2Lt Douglas Woodman, of his formation, said that they had dived on some Huns over Bourlon', McCudden recounted, 'and Maybery got his in flames at once, but whilst firing at it he was leapt on by the "Greentail" Albatros. Then Woodman saw Maybery's machine going down out of control.'

Capt James Thomas Byford McCudden's vivid memoir of his SE 5a flying exploits with No. 56 Sqn included recurring encounters with a green-tailed Albatros that was in fact more than one aircraft from more than one *Staffel*. (Jon Guttman)

Like McCudden, Welsh-born Capt Richard Aveline Maybery had been one of No. 56 Sqn's 'second wave' who carried on the aggressive precedents set by Ball, Crowe, Meintjes and the pioneer SE 5 pilots that they had led. Of the 21 victories credited to him, 19 were Albatros D Vs – including that last one, possibly Ltn Walter Braun of *Jasta* 20, who came down near Faumont at 1405 hrs and died of his wounds at Dourges the next day – thus making Maybery the leading SE 5a ace over that type. The 'Greentail' that Woodman saw attack him was probably Vfw Artur Weber of *Jasta* 5, who was credited with an SE 5a near Havrincourt Wood, although Maybery was also claimed by *K-Flakbatterie* 108, which reported finding his body 600 yards south of Haynecourt.

'Maybery had served some time in the cavalry, the 21st Lancers,' McCudden wrote, 'and he was all for cavalry tactics in the air. He said that whenever Huns were seen they should at once be attacked, and we always argued as to the best way of fighting them in the air. My system was to always attack the Hun at his disadvantage if possible, and if I were attacked at my disadvantage I usually broke off the combat, for in my opinion the Hun in the air must be beaten at his own game, which is cunning.'

On 18 February 1918 McCudden took off at the head of an offensive patrol at 1000 hrs, crossed the lines over Bourlon Wood at 13,000ft and then headed north toward Vitry-en-Artois:

Very soon we sighted a patrol of Albatroses below us climbing up northwards. I signalled the attack to the patrol, and down we went, with the sun behind us. I singled out the leader and fired a good burst from both guns, and I must have riddled the pilot, for he still flew on straight until the machine burst into flames, and it fell over sideways. I got a plain view of the Albatros as it fell away a flaming wreck. It was 'Greentail!' Maybery was avenged! The German pilot had fallen from his machine and was hurtling to destruction faster than his machine.

This Albatros was the identical one that had shot down Maybery in December – it had the green tail, the letter 'K', and the white inverted V across the top of the wing.

I now flew on to the next Albatros and shot him down at once. He dived into the ground north of Vitry, while the flaming 'Greentail' struck the earth just northwest of Vitry. My comrades fought the remaining three Huns, who eventually spun down to safety, and so, as the patrol period came to an end, we flew off home and landed.

Everyone was so bucked about "Greentail" going down that it was all one heard for the rest of the day. However, I must say that the pilot of the green-tailed Albatros must have been a very fine fellow, for during my time on the Cambrai battle front I had many times cause to admire his fighting qualities. I only hope it was my first bullet which killed him. He was German, but he was also a brave man.

Lt Hugh W. L. Saunders (left) of No. 84 Sqn poses with fellow South African Lt Cecil R. Thompson after they downed an LVG C V over Beaurevoir on 18 February 1918 for his second victory. 'Dingbat' Saunders would later add Albatros D Vs to his 15-victory total on 16, 17 and 28 May 1918. (Jon Guttman)

McCudden's detailed description and German records make it possible to determine his opponent on this occasion, and it was not Artur Weber, or even a member of *Jasta* 5! The unfortunate 'Greentail' pilot who fell to earth near Izel-les-Erquerchin, just north of Vitry, was Uffz Julius Kaiser of *Jasta* 35, whose *Staffel* marking was a white chevron across the upper wing and a black chevron below, with different coloured noses and tails, often complemented by the pilot's initials on the fuselage side, as personal markings. The other Albatros, described as having a blue tail, was flown by Uffz Joachim von Stein, who was wounded in the shoulder and mouth. He force-landed his damaged aeroplane and was rushed to *Feldlazarett* Nr 204.

By a remarkable coincidence that led to years of confusion regarding the identity of McCudden's victim, *Jasta* 5 did lose a member to an SE 5a later that same morning. At 1100 hrs, Lt George Owen Johnson was leading a flight from No. 84 Sqn when it encountered some escorted two-seaters over Beaurevoir. Lt Hugh W. L. Saunders (with Lt C. R. Thompson) accounted for an LVG C V in the melee, while Johnson and Lt Percy K. Hobson each claimed an Albatros D V out of control. In this rare case, 'out

ENGAGING THE ENEMY

By the time SE 5s and Albatros D Vs began encountering each other in late June 1917, fighter pilots on both sides had a choice of gunsights. The earliest and simplest involved lining up a bead on a pylon with a ring about three inches in diameter, with four radial wires attached to an inner ring of 0.5-in and 1-in diameter, which allowed for the speed and direction of a moving target, as well as that of the pilot's own aeroplane.

A more sophisticated option was the Aldis sight – a tube that contained a series of lenses marked with two concentric rings, which transmitted parallel light rays. One advantage of this arrangment was that the centre was always directly on the axis of the sight, regardless of the position of the aimer's eye. Both tubes were hermetically sealed to contain an inert gas, which prevented the lenses from fogging. Originally developed by the Aldis brothers in Sparkhill, Birmingham, in 1915 the 32-inch long and 2-inch diameter collimated sight was a mainstay on British fighters. Since neither its Vickers nor Lewis machine guns was in the pilot's direct line of sight, a properly adjusted Aldis sight was an essential item on the SE 5a.

While the collimated tube was useful for the diving hit-and-run tactics at which SE 5a pilots excelled, it was less well regarded by those who preferred to 'mix it up' with the enemy. Harold G. Clements, a six-victory ace in Capt 'Mick' Mannock's A Flight of No. 74 Sqn, recalled the latter making it policy to replace the sights on the scouts in his flight:

'We removed the telescopic Aldis sight and placed the Vickers ring sight on the centreline. This was fixed to the right of the Vickers muzzle and lined up with a bead sight just in front of the winshield. The Aldis was no use at all in our sort of fighting, mostly at extremely close range, and could be made totally useless with oil collecting on the forward lens.'

Clements illustrated his point by describing a swirling, close-in dogfight with a large group of Albatros D Vas and Pfalz D IIIas on 1 June 1918. 'Only rarely did one get the chance to fire, and this is where the point about the telescopic sights comes in. One's eyes had to be everywhere. Enemy aircraft were passing by much too quickly for a pilot to get his eye down to the Aldis and adjust it accordingly. Apart from taking too much time, it kept the eyes away from their very important job of looking about. To get a sight on an enemy aircraft in that way would have been much the same as flying through a mass of stunting machines with one's eyes shut!'

Albatros sights varied from ring and bead to simple tubular sights and, later in 1917, the Oigee gunsight, based on captured Aldis sights, but lacking the inert gas sealed within, resulting in fogged lenses that limited its usefulness. German airmen who preferred the collimated sight sometimes recovered Aldis or French-made Crétien specimens from Allied aeroplanes brought down in their lines for their own use.

Ltn Hans-Joachim von Hippel and his sister Erna pose beside Albatros D V 2065/17, normally flown by *Jasta* 5's commander, Oblt Richard Flashar, but which von Hippel would fly on 18 February 1918. (Greg VanWyngarden)

D V 2065/17 on its back after losing its left lower wing in combat on 18 February 1918. Von Hippel managed to regain control and nurse the aeroplane to a survivable landing, which he could never have done had it been a D Va with the aileron cables routed through the lower wing. (Greg Van Wyngarden)

of control' understated the actual damage done. One of their victims was 22-year-old Vfw Martin Klein, who had served with *Fl Abt* 57 prior to being posted to *Jasta* 5 in November 1917. He perished as a result of Johnson's attack.

The other German, probably credited to Hobson, was Ltn Hans-Joachim von Hippel, whose description of his extraordinary experience in the March 1963 edition of *Jägerblatt* (journal of the German Fighter Pilots' Association) epitomised the danger – and an unexpected benefit – of flying the Albatros D V in combat:

I lost my left lower wing at 4,000 metres altitude at about the same moment that Fw Martin Klein's aircraft (green tail and with the letter 'K' on his wings) passed me into the depths far below with his wings stripped off. Fw Klein had been shot through the head

and his stripped fuselage fell past me at the same instant that I lost my lower left wing. I do not remember anyone shooting at me at that moment because I did not observe any SE 5s behind me. However, since Klein was so close to me and without wings, it would indicate that he had been shot down from above and behind by an SE 5 diving out of the sun.

Our combat commenced at 5,000 metres and I had started a dive down to 4,000 metres without any good reason. When I pulled my stick back and started to level off, my entire left wing became independent of the rest of the aeroplane. The strut did not break, but the mounting rivets on the fuselage, as well as on the 'V' strut, were ripped out so that the wing itself arrived complete and in one part on the ground.

After I had landed and turned over, the wing was found and eventually returned to *Jasta* 5. Upon losing my wings, I immediately turned off the ignition so that the motor could cool and, in case of an impact, the aeroplane would not start to burn – it was my desire to arrive on the ground as a reasonably good-looking body. Klein's machine came down about 1,000 metres from my own wing's landing point, and despite his head wound, he had jumped from his Albatros before the impact and his body was lying close to the wreck.

Besides graphically demonstrating the Albatros D V's structural weakness, von Hippel's account also shows an advantage in the type's aileron arrangement. Had it been a D III or a D Va, the control wires to the ailerons would have gone with his left lower wing. With the controls routed through the D V's upper wing, however, von Hippel was able to maintain some tenuous control of his aeroplane until it turned over upon landing at *Jasta* 5's aerodrome, from which he emerged unhurt. The missing wing was subsequently found at Le Catelet, some 12 miles from Boistrancourt.

Von Hippel received D Va 7037/17 the day after his near-death experience on 18 February, and continued to have his share of mishaps in it. (Greg VanWyngarden)

STATISTICS AND ANALYSIS

In May 1918, as Fokker D VIIs began arriving to replace the Dr I as the tip of the *Luftsteitskräfte's* offensive spear, and ultimately assume the D Va's role as its mainstay, one can only wonder, as James McCudden once did, at how the Germans had held their own as well as they did up to that time. Comparing the rival types in their definitive forms – as the Wolesley Viper-powered SE 5a and the Albatros D Va with the Mercedes IIIa engine – the answer to the question of which was inherently the better fighter remains, by the agreement of pilots on both sides, the SE 5a.

A look at the number of Albatros D Vs credited to SE 5a pilots, in comparison to SE 5as credited to D V pilots, seems to bear that out. There were vastly more of the former, and the type's most successful man, Richard Maybery, was credited with 19 D Vs destroyed, whereas Germany's best, Otto Könnecke, included just four SE 5as among his total of 35. Those two cases, however, embody the essence of why statistics alone are deceptive.

With Albatros scouts dominating the scene, there was little else in the way of active opposition for the SE 5a pilots to fight in 1917 – just the occasional Pfalz D III and the even rarer Fokker Dr I triplane. The Albatros pilots faced a much more varied bag. Besides the SE 5a, they had to know, and deal with, the strengths and weaknesses of the Sopwith Pup, Triplane and Camel, the Bristol F 2B Fighter, the AIRCO DH 5, the Nieuport 17, 23, 24 and 27 and the SPAD VII and XIII. Overriding the question of how to survive encounters with those fighters was another priority – their primary mission of defending their comrades on the ground from reconnaissance aeroplanes, bombers and ground strafers, which had a far greater influence on events in the air.

In consequence the Germans could not possibly specialise in hunting SE 5as, although the more successful pilots accounted for a few amid often impressive overall tallies. While flying Albatros D Vs with *Jasta* 5 between 10 August 1917 and 12 April 1918, for example, Könnecke's 14 accredited victories included four RE 8s, three DH 5s, two Camels and a Sopwith 1½ Strutter, as well as the four SE 5as. Only one of the eight British aircraft downed by Manfred von Richthofen while flying D Vs was an SE 5a, the rest being three RE 8s, two SPAD VIIs, a Nieuport 23 and a DH 5.

There was another reason why SE 5as figured so relatively sparsely in Albatros aces' scores. Whereas the pilot of a nimble, but slow, Camel or Nieuport caught at a disadvantage had little option but to fight his way out, an SE 5a pilot enjoyed good odds of escaping in a dive. If he did so, the pursuing Albatros pilot usually had only seconds to get in a fatal shot before his quarry widened the range – and the *Jagdflieger* would be wise to break off his pursuit as soon as he felt that lower wing start to buffet.

Those factors may be reflected in German claims against British aeroplanes from June through to December 1917, when the D V was their primary mount. Some 885 RFC and RNAS machines were claimed by the *Jastas*, but only 52 of these were SE 5/5as – against which known SE 5/5a pilot casualties actually totalled just 37.

Since they were mostly fighting over the enemy side of the lines, British claims were much more inflated, although the fraction of casualties that turn up in German records show that they were taking an almost daily toll. Those losses, however, were equally proportionate to the other British fighters they engaged, with a goodly amount falling victim to Camels, Bristol Fighters, Pups, Nieuports, SPADs and even two-seater bomber and reconnaissance types, as well as SE 5/5as.

Gwilym Hugh Lewis, who was credited with two victories in DH 2s with No. 32 Sqn and ten flying SE 5as in No. 40 Sqn, explained the RFC's scoring rationale in a letter home on 21 January 1918:

Another view of the two No. 84 Sqn SE 5as at *Jasta* 17's airfield as seen on page 63 – B544 'E', flown by 2Lt George R. Gray, mortally wounded by Ltn Erwin Böhme of *Jasta* 'Boelcke' on 31 October 1917, and B566 'J', in which 2Lt A. W. Rush had been brought down and captured three days earlier. (Greg VanWyngarden)

Among the few of Capt William A. Bishop's 72 victories that can be traced to an identifiable German loss, an Albatros D V he claimed in flames over Hendicourt at 2000 hrs on 5 August 1917 corresponds to the death of Ltn Burkhardt Lehmann of *Jasta* 12. However, his squadronmates Capt William E. Molesworth and Lt Spencer B. Horn also shared in another 'flamer' at the same time. (Smithsonian Institution 85-12303)

A Hun out of control is one brought down over the frontlines, which is seen by several people and is considered certain to ground observers, or else breaks up or flames. Hence the disadvantage of fighting over the frontlines where a scrap is never seen.

Lewis' only Albatros D V was credited to him as out of control on 19 January 1918 during a typical encounter, which started with three SE 5as versus five D Vs. They were subsequently joined by three more Albatros, another patrol of SE 5as and, finally, four Camels. Then, Lewis wrote, the Germans reached their 'time limit' and began to disengage. 'I saw only three above, and they were climbing away. I believe they climb better than we do, though we are a good deal faster. The SEs then went south and the Camels to the north.' For their part, the Germans credited ten-victory ace Ltn Karl Gallwitz of *Jasta* 'Boelcke' with an 'SE 5' downed south of the Houthulst Forest, although the only British loss in the fight was 2Lt E T Baker of No. 65 Sqn – in a Camel!

Robert L. Chidlaw-Roberts, who preferred not to be called an ace despite claiming ten victories, was a former FE 2b pilot of No. 18 Sqn who flew SE 5as with Nos. 60 and 40 Sqns. He long remembered his second victory, on 16 September 1917, which corresponded to the death of Ltn Alfred Bauer of *Jasta* 17:

I was firing on one, an Albatros I think, and it just blew up into little bits. I've never seen it before or since, and it nearly made me sick. That was the first one I'd shot down that I really knew I'd got.

Albatros D V pilots known to have gone down to SE 5as' guns often have to be filtered out from multiple claims. For example, in one scrap on 5 August 1917 Capt W. A. Bishop of No. 60 Sqn claimed an Albatros in flames at 2000 hrs and another out of control 20 minutes later, both between Hendicourt and Moncy. Credit for a second 'flamer' over Hendicourt at 2000 hrs was shared by Capt William E. Molesworth and Lt Spencer B. Horn. Against those three claims, *Jasta* 12 recorded the death of Ltn Burkhardt Lehmann over Hendicourt at 2040 hrs.

Apparently, the first German ace to die in a D V at the hands of an SE 5 fell on 16 July 1917, when four No. 56 Sqn aeroplanes fought 15 Albatros whose dive and zoom tactics drove the fight down from 14,000ft to 4,000 ft until Capt Bowman got on one 'V-strutter's' tail and fired a long burst. He saw it dive, engine full on, and crash at the eastern end of the race couse in Polygon Wood. His victim was Vfw Fritz Krebs, who, since joining *Jasta* 6, had scored eight victories in three months.

Jasta 26 seems to have fought No. 60 Sqn on 22 September 1917, and after the engagement Oblt Bruno Loerzer claimed a 'Camel' at 1015 hrs, which was more likely the SE 5a of Lt James Whiting, who was killed. At 1035 hrs Lt Ian Macgregor also force-landed in Allied lines with a leg wound, but ten minutes later Capts Chidlaw-Roberts and Harold A. Hamersley were jointly credited with a green and black Albatros 'driven down out of control' southeast of Zonnebeke. Their victim in this case was Off Stv Fritz Kosmahl, a nine-victory ace from *Jasta* 26 who landed south of Poelkapelle with a stomach wound, from which he died in hospital on the 26th.

'Fighting Fifty-Six' struck again on 28 September, when Reg Hoidge shot a D V down in pieces west of Westroosebecke and Bowman sent another down in a dive until it disintegrated in mid-air. *Jasta* 3 recorded the death of Ltn Kurt Wissemann (whose five victories included – falsely, it turns out – French ace Capitaine Georges Guynemer) and the downing of ace Ltn Karl Menckhoff, who survived.

Two *Jasta* 26 aces subsequently figured in the deaths of No. 56 Sqn aces Lt Robert H. Sloley, who had nine victories to his name when Ltn Xaver Dannhuber killed him on 1 October, and Lt Charles H. Jeffs, who had scored his fifth on 29 September and was killed by Bruno Loerzer on 5 October. An even worse loss to No. 56 Sqn occurred on 27 October, when 2Lt A. P. F. Rhys Davids, whose 25 victories included Werner Voss, was killed by ace Ltn Karl Gallwitz of *Jasta* 'Boelcke'.

Another case of multi-claiming concerned the death of Ltn Max *Ritter* von Müller, victor over 38 Allied aeroplanes and newly appointed acting commander of *Jasta* 'Boelcke', on 9 January 1918. At 1250 hrs he had closed to within 25 yards of the RE 8 piloted by Capt George F. W. Zimmer of No. 21 Sqn when the observer, 2Lt Harry A. Somerville, shot him down over Moorsele, Müller jumping or falling from his burning Albatros D V 5405/17. As he attacked the RE 8, however, aces Capts R. L. Chidlaw-Roberts and F. O. Soden of No. 60 Sqn were diving to the two-seater's rescue, firing at the Albatros from above and behind. They consequently shared credit in the Bavarian ace's demise.

Jasta 10 was operating a mixed bag of Albatros D Vas and Pfalz D IIIs in early 1918, but Ltn Max Kuhn seems to have been flying the former when he got a damaging hit into an SE 5a's engine on 2 February. His opponent, who force-landed and was taken prisoner, turned out to be Maj Frederick J. Powell, a pioneer ace who

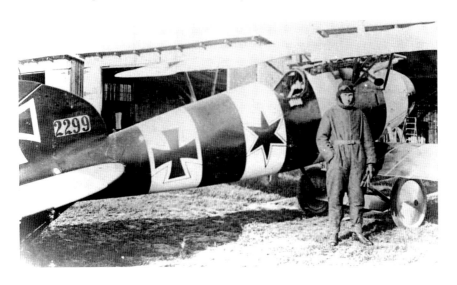

Ltn Xavier Dannhuber beside Albatros D V 2299/17 in black and white *Jasta* 26 livery. Dannhuber's 11 victories included Lt Robert H. Sloley, a nine-victory ace of No. 56 Sqn whom he shot down and killed on 1 October 1917. Four days later, Dannhuber's *Staffelführer*, Oblt Bruno Loerzer, killed Lt Charles H. Jeffs of No. 56 Sqn, who had scored his fifth victory on 29 September. (Jon Guttman)

was credited with six victories in Vickers FB 5s and FE 8s in 1915–16. He had failed to add to his tally since taking command of No. 41 Sqn on 2 August 1917.

After the Germans launched the *Kaiserschlacht* offensive, Fokker Dr Is flown by the cream of the *Jagdflieger* tended to dominate the dogfights, but the British occasionally lost a prominent man to the odd Albatros or even a Pfalz. Capt Kelvin Crawford, a five-victory ace on DH 2s who had newly returned in SE 5as with

Leading SE 5/SE 5a Albatros D V/Va Killers			
Pilot	Squadron(s)	D V/Vas	Total
Richard A. Maybery	56	19	21
Geoffrey H. Bowman	56	15	32
Reginald T. C. Hoidge	56	14	28
Anthony W. Beauchamp Proctor	84	13	54
Arthur P. F. Rhys Davids	56	13	25
Leonard M. Barlow	56	12+1 shared	20
William A. Bishop	60	12	72
James T. B. McCudden	56	12	57
George E. H. McElroy	40 & 24	11	46
Gerald J. C. Maxwell	56	10	26
James A. Slater	64	9	24
Frederick E. Brown	84	8	10
Frederick R. G. McCall	41	8	35
Frank O. Soden	60 & 41	8	27
Percy J. Clayson	1	7	29
Harold A. Hamersley	60	7	13
Edward Mannock	40, 74 & 85	7	61
Robert H. Sloley	56	7	9
Kenneth W. Junor	56	6	8
Kenneth M. StC G. Leask	84	6	8
Ian D. R. McDonald	24	6	20
Gerald G. Bell	150	5	16
Robert L. Chidlaw-Roberts	60 & 40	5	10
William J. A. Duncan	60	5	11
William L. Harrison	40 & 1	5	12
Herbert G. Hegarty	60	5	8
Richard W. Howard	2 AFC	5	8
Hector O. MacDonald	84	5	7
Edmund R. Tempest	64	5	17

No. 60 Sqn, was killed on 11 April by Ltn Könnecke of *Jasta* 5. On the same day No. 56 Sqn's Lt Henry J. Walkerdine was driven down wounded in British lines after losing a head-on gun duel with 17-victory ace Ltn Walter Böning of *Jasta* 76b. His damaged SE 5a was later restored to airworthiness and Walkerdine subsequently survived the war with seven victories to his name.

Among the last British aces to die in an SE 5a at the hands of an Albatros was Maj Edwin L. Benbow, who had actually scored all eight of his victories with No. 40 Sqn in FE 8s – the only pilot to 'make ace' exclusively in that type. In May 1918 Benbow returned to the front as a flight leader in No. 85 Sqn, but like Crawford he had to familiarise himself with the new, faster-paced nature of aerial combat. Before he could do so, Benbow was killed over Nieppe Forest on 30 May by eight-victory ace Oblt Hans-Eberhardt Gandert, CO of *Jasta* 51.

When it comes to the SE 5a and the Albatros D V, and most World War I fighters for that matter, statistics become secondary to the human factor. Comparisons really need to be based on combat experiences, and these could vary widely.

The diminutive Bavarian Ltn Max *Ritter* von Müller, victor over 38 Allied aeroplanes and newly appointed acting commander of *Jasta* 'Boelcke', fell on 9 January 1918. His demise was credited to both an RE 8 crew and SE 5a aces Capts R. L. Chidlaw-Roberts and F. O. Soden of No. 60 Sqn. (Greg VanWyngarden)

'Compared to the Albatros, the SE 5a might have been slightly faster,' Chidlaw-Roberts opined. 'We didn't think much of the Pfalz, as it didn't have the speed or climb, although I was shot down by one and landed near our frontline – I had taken a hole in my sump and had to come down. A fighter's effectiveness all depended on who was flying it. A first class pilot could fly almost anything, but we never really worried about the Pfalz or the Albatros – not like the triplanes or the new Fokker D VIIs that came out later'.

Leading Albatros D V/Va SE 5/5a Killers

Pilot	*Jasta(s)*	SE 5/5as	Total
Otto Könnecke	5	4	35
Emil Koch	12 & 32	3	7
Bruno Loerzer	26	3	44
Karl Menckhoff	3 & 72s	3	39
Eduard *Ritter* von Schleich	JGr 8	3	35

AFTERMATH

In the weeks just prior to Operation *Kaiserschlacht*, the RFC's fighter force primarily consisted of Sopwith Camels and SE 5as, supplemented by Bristol F 2Bs and a remnant of SPADs and Nieuports. Germany's most numerous fighter, in spite of its flaws from the outset, remained the Albatros D V and its reinforced scion the D Va, backing up a small vanguard of Fokker Dr Is and a complement of Pfalz D IIIs and D IIIas.

Manfred von Richthofen, who had so looked forward to seeing his *Geschwader* obtain Fokker D VIIs, had 80 victories and was still flying a Dr I when he was killed on 21 April 1918. At the end of the month, the German fighter inventory on the Western Front comprised 928 Albatros D Vas, 174 D IIIs and 131 D Vs, along with 433 Pfalz D IIIas, 171 Fokker Dr Is and 19 Fokker D VIIs.

From the end of May 1918, however, Germany's most ubiquitous fighter became the Fokker D VII. Its numbers – never sufficient in the eyes of the *Jagdflieger* – were

Jasta 27 ground crewmen manhandle an Albatros D Va on Halluin-Ost aerodrome in May 1918, even while the unit was primarily operating Fokker Dr Is and looking forward, hopefully, toward soon getting D VIIs. (Greg VanWyngarden)

Although SE 5as did not remain long in RAF service after the war, the US Army acquired parts for 56 aeroplanes, assembled by the Eberhart Steel Products Company with plywood-skinned fuselages and powered by American-built 180hp Wright-Hispano 'E' engines. Designated SE 5Es, they served as fighter trainers into the mid-1920s. (Jon Guttman)

compensated for by less-desired Roland D VIs and Pfalz D VIIIs and D XIIs, superb but mechanically temperamental SSW D IIIs and D IVs and remaining stocks of Fokker Dr Is, Albatros D Vas and Pfalz D IIIas. The last German fighter inventory, compiled on 31 August 1918, indicated that 307 Albatros D Vas, 52 D IIIs and 20 D Vs were still operational, although most of them were soldiering on in *Amerikaprogramm* or home defence units, pending the availability of newer types.

From the time the RFC and RNAS merged into the RAF on 1 April 1918, its fighter mainstays remained the SE 5a, Camel and Bristol F 2B Fighter, complemented by Sopwith Dolphins and, later, Snipes. Significantly, however, while the *Jagdflieger* viewed the Fokker D VII as a long-overdue upgrade over the Albatros, SE 5a and Camel pilots found themselves at least holding their own against Germany's newest and best, even though their proven single-seat warhorses had made their debuts many months before the D VII – in April and June 1917, respectively.

Both British types had roughly the same strengths to pit against the Fokker as they had had against the Albatros D Va – the Camel could still out-manoeuvre the D VII and the SE 5a could still out-dive it. For their part, the Fokker pilots did their best to cancel out the enemy's strengths, just as the Albatros pilots had done before them. In the D VII's case, however, the disparity in both manoeuvrability and speed between it and both of its principal British counterparts was considerably less marked than it had been for the Albatros.

And so the struggle continued to the Armistice of 11 November 1918, with Allied numbers inexorably forcing the Germans into a fighting retreat on land and in the air, but the *Jagdflieger* remaining defiant to the end. As circumstance would have it, even those last days still saw the occasional Albatros D Va gamely rise to challenge its old adversary of 1917, the SE 5a.

Albatros D Va 7161/17 is believed to have been landed in Allied lines near Marcelcave by Uffz Erich Gurgenz of *Jasta* 46 on 4 April 1918 after he had been mortally wounded, and claimed by (but not officially credited to) Adjudant Paul Petit of *Escadrille* SPA154. Fully restored in 1979, the scout is currently on display at the National Air and Space Museum in Washington, DC. (Jon Guttman)

FURTHER READING

BOOKS

Bishop, William A., *Winged Warfare* (ARCO Publishing Inc., 1981)

Bruce, J. M., *Windsock Datafile 30 – RAF SE 5* (Albatros Productions Ltd, 1991)

Franks, Norman and Bailey, Frank W., *Above the Lines* (Grub Street, 1993)

Franks, Norman, Bailey, Frank and Duiven, Rick, *The Jasta War Chronology* (Grub Street, 1998)

Gray, Peter, *The Albatros D V* (Profile Publications Ltd, 1965

Grosz, Peter M., *Albatros Experimentals* (Albatros Productions Ltd, 1992)

Kilduff, Peter, *Richthofen – Beyond the Legend of the Red Baron* (Arms & Armour Press, 1993)

Lewis, Wg Cdr Gwilym H. DFC, *Wings over the Somme, 1916–1918* (William Kimber & Co Ltd, 1976)

McCudden, Maj James T. B., *Flying Fury – Five Years in the Royal Flying Corps* (Ace Publishing Corp, 1968)

Merrill, G. K., *Jagdstaffel 5*, Vols 1 and 2 (Albatros Productions Ltd, 2004)

Revell, Alex, *High in the Empty Blue – The History of No 56 Sqn RFC/RAF 1916–1919* (Flying Machines Press, 1995)

Revell, Alex, *British Single-Seater Fighter Squadrons on the Western Front in World War I* (Schiffer Publishing Ltd, 2006)

Rimell, Raymond Laurence, *Windsock Datafile 3 – Albatros D V* (Albatros Productions Ltd, 1987)

Shores, Christopher, Franks, Norman and Guest, Russell, *Above the Trenches* (Grub Street, 1990)

MAGAZINES

Chidlaw-Roberts, Robert Leslie, MC, RAF, and Tappin, David, 'Chidlaw – Just an Ordinary Humdrum Pilot', *Cross & Cockade International Journal*, Vol. 20, No. 2, pp.57–67 (Autumn 1987)

Daniel, Walter Campbell, 'Recollections of a World War 1 Flyer, Royal Flying Corps/Royal Air Force, 1917–1918', *Cross & Cockade Great Britain*, Vol. 2, No. 2, pp.56–62 (Summer 1971)

Dudgeon, James M., '"Clem", 1893–1983, Lt Harris G. Clements, Alberta Regiment attached to RFC & RAF No 74 Sqn', *Cross & Cockade International Journal*, Vol. 18, No. 3, pp.131–135 (Autumn 1987)

Grosz, Peter M., 'The Agile & Aggressive Albatros', *Air Enthusiast Quarterly*, No 1, pp.36–51

Osten, Hans-Georg von der, 'With *Jagdstaffeln* 11 and 4', *Cross & Cockade (USA) Journal*, Vol. 15, No. 3, pp.219–226 (Autumn 1974)

Puglisi, W. G., 'Letters from German *Jagdstaffel* Personnel of World War I', *Cross & Cockade (USA) Journal*, Vol. 1, No. 1, p.39 (Spring 1960)

Russell, H. H., 'Capt R. A. Maybery MC and Bar', *Cross & Cockade (USA) Journal*, Vol. 14, No. 2, pp.131–149 (Summer 1973)

Scheidig, Max, 'Life in the *Jagdstaffel*', *Cross & Cockade (USA) Journal*, Vol. 13, No. 2, pp.128–149 (Summer 1972)

Tutschek, Adolf *Ritter* von, 'The War Letters of Hptm Adolf *Ritter* von Tutschek', *Over the Front*, Vol. 3, No. 4 (Winter 1988) and Vol. 4, No. 1 (Spring 1989)

INDEX